From Where I Stand

End Time Issues As I See Them

Don McGee

June 2012

Copyright © by Don McGee

ISBN: 978-0-9794659-1-8

Library of Congress Control Number: 2012911402

Cover design by Jacob Jolibois / *Jacob Thomas Imagery*

All Scripture quotations, unless otherwise noted, are from the New American Standard Bible © 1995 by the Lockman Foundation. Used by permission.

But know this: difficult times will
come in the last days.
--2 Timothy 3:1 (HCSB)

Crown & Sickle Ministries
60498 Floyd Rd.
Amite, LA 70422
www.crownandsickle.org

*Hope for the Christian is the imminent return of
Jesus. Nothing more, nothing less, nothing else.*

Dedication

This book is dedicated to the late Stanford Broussard, preacher for 58 years at the Bayou Jacque Church of Christ near Big Cane, Louisiana. He was a friend, encourager and mentor whose impact is indelibly stamped in my life. His regular and literal emphasis upon the prophetic scriptures in general and the Blessed Hope in particular prepared my heart and mind for my life's work.

It is imminent.

Preface

Most books are written with a specific subject in mind, and that subject is laid out in a manner that allows the reader to clearly see what the author has to say about it.

This book, however, is a compilation of a number of articles whose association with each other is their relevance to the end time as seen from a biblical perspective. They include politics, economics, religions, Jews, Gentiles, cultures and others. The chapters in this book reflect my viewpoint on some of them.

No single topic is treated to the point of exhaustion, and no attempt has been made to do so. Only the more obvious peaks protruding from the mountain range of end time issues are addressed. Thus, with each succeeding chapter the reader's attention is redirected toward another issue relevant to this dying world and our returning Savior.

Bible students are well aware of God's revelation of the course of human history. From the Garden to the eternal state, He has given humanity a synopsis of creation, rebellion, redemption and eternity. Much of what His inspired writers have given us is written in generalities allowing both the passing of time and prayerful study to illuminate some of the details. Other things, however, have been given to us in amazing clarity, and strangely enough it is often those events that are soundly rejected by most of the church. Occasionally, some of the reasons for this rejection are mentioned.

We are not left in utter confusion in our effort to discern some of those details. By using the Bible's template to interpret current events students are able to see more clearly where the human race is presently on the timeline of history. And, with the passing of time that picture often evolves into clearer focus.

There are several obstacles that must be overcome in order to achieve a clear picture. Perhaps foremost is the tendency for the church to interpret current world events using the religiously-correct, but mistaken premise that God is finished with the Jewish people. This is commonly referred to as replacement theology, and is taught in most seminary classrooms and from most pulpits.

A second obstacle, and closely related to the first, is the non-literal interpretation of prophetic scripture. Various writing styles inspired by the Holy Spirit have been used in the compilation of the Bible including hyperbole, allegory and simile. Yet, no such use of those styles should cause any student to overlook or deny their obvious and clearly-intended meaning.

Further, the adoption of a vitriolic attitude toward those with whom one might disagree is not only a hindrance to seeing prophecy clearly, but also perverts the relationship God expects His people to have with each other. Such an attitude must at all times be avoided.

"End time issues as I see them". The operative phrase is "as I see them". What the reader finds in this book are my views on a variety of issues associated with these last days of the church age. Because of this it is important to keep a couple of things in mind. First, what is presented here is my fallible view of some of those scriptures in context of current events.

Second, world events inherently change very quickly, and with each day comes new information regarding those events and how they relate to prophecy. The way something looks today might not be the way it looks tomorrow. The point of the spear, however, in all things written in this book is the imminent return of Jesus for His church. Maranatha!

Contents

Chapter 1

A Snapshot of The Jew

~ ~ ~ ~ ~

Any attempt to understand the global political climate without a fundamental understanding of the Jew is not only an exercise in futility, but is dangerous. Futile because the past, present and future of humanity are all eternally tethered to God's call of Abraham, and dangerous because ignorance is one of Satan's most effective means of fostering anti-Semitism, which is repugnant in the nostrils of God and which incurs His blazing wrath.

The Root of the Jew

The beginning of the Hebrew people goes back to Genesis 12, but events prior to that time figure prominently into the reason for Abraham's call and the founding of the Jewish race. Because of humanity's utter spiritual depravity God destroyed the entire population of the earth with a worldwide deluge excepting Noah and seven others.

But, once again man refused to live as God had commanded and eventually migrated back to the Plain of Shinar (Babylon) insisting upon maintaining an autonomous culture free from God's plan and purpose. The result was a repeat of the situation that caused the flood just a little over 300 years earlier.

Now, what was God to do? Destroy the world with water again? No, a world-wide deluge would not do because He promised that would never happen again. So, what's the plan? It is recorded in Genesis 12.

At the close of Genesis 11 there were many nation-families that descended from Noah, and each was becoming increasingly wicked. If God were to keep His promise to not destroy the world again in spite of its moral decline, and if He were to keep the promise He made in Genesis 3:15, He would have to form a separate nation-family through which He would bring salvation to the human race. This family would of necessity be different, and its blood-line would have to be rooted in a man who was different from all other men of his day. He would have to be a man of great faith, which means he would have to not only know about God, but would have to actually know Him and have complete faith in what He told him without regard to visible circumstances.

As the eye of God scanned the known world of that time it came to rest, as the star upon Bethlehem 2000 years later, on the city of Ur, in modern Iraq. And, among its citizens was just such a man, Abram, son of Terah. Without explanation God commanded him to leave his native country, his people and his family and go to place He would show him later. God also promised Abram that he would father a great nation, that he would become great, that he would be especially blessed by God and that the entire world would benefit from his life and descendants. The Jewish nation is framed.

Confirmation by a Miracle

So, how could Abram know this was of God, and not simply the result of events spun from his own subconscious mind and played out in a series of coincidences? Further, how can the modern reader also know? As is often the case, God signs off on His special purposes with His signature in the form of a miracle. To any unbiased observer His autograph appears many times on the pages of human history. But, this particular endorsement came in the form of Isaac being born to Abraham when he was 100 years old and Sarah was 90. Lo, the first fully Jewish baby is born.

The Nation is Tempered

God repeated the same promise to Isaac and to his son Jacob so that Abraham's family would understand the covenant-promise was both unconditional and everlasting. Abraham's grandson was Jacob (whose name was changed to Israel by God), and he fathered 12 sons whose descendants would eventually become the 12 Hebrew Tribes. But, they and their less than 80 family members were not ready for the task ahead. Certain things had to be done; things that were as necessary as they were painful.

As Moses records the early history of this special family that God had inaugurated, it became clear that this family had to be prepared by special experiences in order to produce a unique culture and lineage from which Messiah-Savior would come. Jacob and his family lived in Canaan (not Palestine!) among some of the most pagan tribes that ever populated the earth. The first thing God had to do was to separate them from the influence of the heathens of Canaan and forge them into a nation in another place, all while at the same time keeping them separate from the pagan influences of their new hosts. The answer was Egypt.

In Genesis 15 God briefly outlined His plan to Abraham, but did not offer many details. God used the kidnapping of Joseph and a famine in Canaan to get Jacob and his family into Egypt. Because they were shepherds and thus despised by the Egyptians, they were left alone in Goshen to grow into a vast multitude, about 2 million strong. Their numbers became a threat to the Egyptians, and for this reason they were enslaved for 400 years. It was the fires of slavery that caused them to want to leave Egypt; something very similar to the fires of persecution in WW2 that caused them to leave Europe in order to reestablish their ancient nation of Israel in their own homeland.

The Nation Gets an Identity

In Genesis 17 God established a means of covenant-identification with Abraham and his descendants. At age 8 days every male was to be circumcised. This rite brought them into something of a covenant-fellowship that included only the Jews, their slaves and those foreigners who chose to join the Hebrew nation. Though circumcision was practiced among other groups such as the Moabites and Edomites — but not among the Canaanites and Philistines — yet, for the Jews it was a distinguishing feature because it was part of God's covenant with them.

On the way from Egypt to Canaan God established another means of bringing them into full separation from the world at large while in the process of "Hebrew-izing" them. This was done by instituting another covenant, this one different from the Abrahamic Covenant in that it was based upon law with conditional blessings — the Mosaic Covenant.

The imposition of the Law brought the Jews into a religious relationship with God, and prescribed specific ordinances and rituals that were to be practiced. The pagans of Canaan had religion with certain laws that dictated the way they related to their idol gods. But, among the things that distinguished the Hebrews from the pagans was that their legal relationship was with the sole, singular God while the pagans worshipped grotesque and dead idols of wood, stone and metal; a kind of worship that required the sacrifice of their children among other things. Even the thought of such sacrifices was never in the mind of God.

The Preservation of the Jews

No other people-group in history has seen hardship like the Jews. Moses issued a detailed warning to his people regarding what they could expect in the future. How accurate! *Moreover, the Lord will scatter you among all peoples, from one end of the earth to the other end of the earth; and there you shall serve other gods, wood and stone, which you or your fathers have not known. And among those nations you shall find no rest, and there shall be no resting place for the sole of your foot; but there the Lord will give you a trembling heart, failing of eyes, and despair of soul. So your life shall hang in doubt before you; and you shall be in dread night and day, and shall have no assurance of your life* (Deuteronomy 28:64-66 NASB).

Persecution has been part of being Jewish from the beginning until this very day. We think of the atrocities against the Jews during the 12-year Holocaust, and they were indeed horrendous. But, what is often ignored is the fact that Islam has been at war against the Jews since their 7th century Islamic crusades in which untold multitudes were slaughtered in Arabia, North Africa and Europe. And, in these last days such hatred for the Jew has not been abated.

But, in spite of this the Jew has been preserved. From Pharaoh until today her enemies have been consigned to the ash heap of history because God's unconditional promises will not allow her destruction. The Jews have not been spared annihilation because they are inherently more deserving than anybody else, but because God made an unconditional promise to them regarding these matters, and His name's honor will not be discredited (Ezekiel 36:22).

There is yet one more reason the Jews will forever retain their distinct identity. They cannot be assimilated into any host culture. With few exceptions, an immigrant family is fully assimilated into a host culture by the third generation. Not so with Jews. We hear of Irish-Americans and Asian-Americans, but never Jewish-Americans. Rather, we hear of American Jews. They have been kept from being lost in the Gentile world because their distinction is part of God's purpose for their existence.

One of the first defenses German Jews used at the beginning of the Nazi persecutions was that they were Germans, with many even touting their service to the Fatherland during the first world war. They might have thought they were Germans, but Hitler taught them they were Jews. The same is true in every country in the world today.

Israel

After being shot, gassed, crucified, burned alive and murdered in every way imaginable the Jewish people reclaimed their ancient homeland in 1948. God said He would bring them back, and He did.

I believe among the most important places to visit in all Israel are the Temple Mt. area, Bethlehem, the Mt. of Olives, the Garden Tomb, the Valley of Jezreel and Independence Hall in Tel Aviv. Why Independence Hall? Because that is where David Ben-Gurion declared Israel a nation again in 1948. Yet, it is the most neglected place of all, in spite of the fact Bible prophecy was fulfilled in that very room in our lifetime.

Why is it neglected? Why do tour leaders avoid it? Because the overwhelming majority of Christians, their churches and their religious leaders flat-out refuse to acknowledge the literal importance of Bible prophecy, and its incalculable role in the entire world's geo-political course. To visit Israel and not see, touch, smell and take in this room with every sense available is to greatly lessen the benefit of such a trip.

Yes, the land is theirs. And, yes, they will never be removed from it again. But, Oh, the cost that is coming! God has brought the Jew back to the land He gave them, and they will be there...particularly in Jerusalem...when Jesus comes for the second time to this earth at the Mt. of Olives. His coming will be in response to their almost total annihilation as 66% will die at the hands of anti-Christ and a totally anti-Semitic world. Jewish blood will be as cheap and as plentiful as the rocks that fill that embattled land. And, it is at that point that they will finally accept their Messiah.

But, the Lord guarantees their survival as a nation, just like He promised Abraham several millennia in the past. Their enemies will fall like flies as Jesus destroys them in the most withering blitzkrieg in human history. The death of the enemies of the Jews is described in a most dramatic way: their skin, eyes and tongues will rot before their bodies even hit the ground (Zechariah 14).

Any snapshot of the Jews would be incomplete without God's warning...*For thus says the Lord of hosts, "After glory He has sent me against the nations which plunder you, for he who touches you, touches the apple (pupil) of His eye"* (Zechariah 2:8 NASB).

Nothing gets one's attention like a foreign object touching the eye. Said another way, it would be wise for any king, president, nation, religion...whatever or whoever...to remember that only a fool provokes God. DLM

Chapter 2

Laodicea—Assuming Room Temperature
~ ~ ~ ~ ~

Years ago in a college class on forensic methods we studied the various techniques used to determine how long a human body has been dead. The methods are many and are often somewhat complicated, but one basic technique is to contrast the environmental temperature with the temperature of the deceased. The point is to see how close the body temperature of the deceased is to the ambient (room) temperature. A dead body, you see, will take on the temperature of its environment. Such was the case with the church at Laodicea.

Laodicea can be loosely translated "mob rule". It was the democratic church where popular opinion was the law, and the concept of what is right or wrong was voted upon. Jesus had nothing good to say about it. The church was ineffective and dead.

In Revelation 3:14ff Jesus described the Laodicean church as "lukewarm"; that is, it was neither hot nor cold. Basically it was at room temperature and was thus nauseating and worthy of being vomited out of His mouth. He wanted the church to be either "hot" or "cold" with both terms meaning being different from the world around them and thus capable of having an impact. Being "hot" does not mean being "on fire" and being "cold" does not mean being "dead"; they are both positive terms that describe something that is desirable such as hot coffee or cold water. Laodicea was a church that allowed itself to be overly influenced by the world around it with the obvious result being that it lost its godly influence. It was death by Satan's very effective one/two punch: spiritual impotence and worldly association.

Laodicea, being the last of the seven churches mentioned, is often seen as representing many in the church at the end of the age just before Jesus returns for His bride. We are living in that age and many in the church are indeed lukewarm and severely influenced by the world around them. In fact, though there is some semblance of religion associated with such people, the fact of the matter is that deep down the modern Laodiceans are not much different from the secular world around them.

We know the church will not be destroyed and we know the gates of hell will not prevail against her. But, we also know the church is susceptible to error, heresy and worldly influence. We are warned about wolves in sheep's clothing, about false teachers and other dangers that threaten the sanctity and purity of the church. So, what characteristics might be playing a role in deadening the impact of the church in these last days? Is there anything we can watch out for? I think so.

Health and Wealth Gospel

The Laodicean city fathers thought their city was in good shape. They were rich, you see. They were so rich that the local banking system financed the reconstruction of the city in A.D. 60, after an earthquake destroyed it, without aid from Rome. This was a matter of great pride for the Laodiceans. That area produced an expensive glossy black wool for which the city was famous. They had something of a medical school along with a drug company that manufactured a famous eye-salve. They thought they were independent and needed nothing from anyone. They were progressive, self-sufficient and very wealthy.

What city could want more?

The church in Laodicea should have had a message for their arrogant fellow citizens, but the message somehow got lost as the church took on the prideful and wealth-oriented characteristics of the city. Money seemed to solve all problems. Have you ever been in a church business meeting where the main thing was the financial report, and if the money situation was good then the church must surely be doing okay spiritually?

The modern "name-it-and-claim-it" preachers are having a hayday these days. One in particular will put on "Holy Spirit demonstrations of power" on a large stage in front of thousands. People go to those meetings with their problems and leave their money with the evangelist in appreciation for expected health and wealth. We wonder why Paul didn't know about all this when Timothy and Epaphroditus were sick, and why he didn't tell the churches in Judea about this when they suffered so much during a famine. Funny thing about those name-it-and-claim-it guys — we don't see them preaching the health/wealth gospel to twelve or fifteen people in the dirt-poor leper infested neighborhoods of Calcutta. Does anybody wonder why?

As a result of this materialistic focus the Laodicean church of the end times chooses her leadership as corporate American chooses hers. The result is a church that has forgotten her message and is more concerned about positive public perception, materialism and showmanship than truth, fidelity and evangelism.

Downplaying of Doctrine

We have probably all heard people say, "Doctrine divides; love unites". They say this as if to mean doctrine and love are mutually exclusive — you either have to focus on doctrine or love. These same people often have trouble reconciling the grace of Romans and the works of James. The fact is all doctrines and principles in the Bible are interrelated and cannot be divided.

The Jesus that said, "Love one another" is the same Jesus that said, "Except you..."

Modern Laodicean churches, who believe love is the same as tolerance, are long on broadmindedness and short on doctrine. They desire reputations for being open-minded about those things that divide people. To the modern Laodicean church, what a person believes about basic Bible doctrines regarding Jesus, salvation, the Holy Spirit, eternity, etc. are not important as long as everybody gets along and loves everybody else. They forget that Jesus once said, *Do not think that I came to bring peace on the earth; I did not come to bring peace, but a sword. For I came to set a man against his father, and a daughter against her mother, and a daughter-in-law against her mother-in-law; and a man's enemies will be the members of his household* (Matthew 10:34-36 NASB). Jesus does, in fact, divide people. In fact, He is the greatest divider the world has ever known.

Very seldom, if ever, do modern preachers expound doctrinal texts such as relate to divorce, morality, love of money, hell, etc. These texts, though a definite part of God's word, are purposefully avoided because they "divide people and hurt their feelings". It is better, they say, to talk about things that unite like tolerance, getting a positive self image, the psychology of sin from a modern perspective and other such things that make people feel better about themselves.

The apostate church of Revelation 17 will be very inclusive and ecumenical. It will accept just about anyone as a member — as long as biblical truth is not part of their belief system. Even then the mantra could be, "Doctrine divides; love unites".

Unbiblical Portrayal of God

The God of the Bible is not the god of the Laodicean and modern apostate church. Unitarians, New Agers and others portray God as a doting old grandfather who will send no one to hell and will allow everyone into heaven. Their god is all-inclusive, tolerant and demands no doctrinal requisites from his followers because he does not label any conduct as actual sin. Every word, thought or deed is to be labeled, defined and dealt with on a sliding scale of mitigating circumstances. Therefore, nothing is really sin because everything is relative.

The truth is their god is no god at all. He is a figment of their imagination; an idol created by their own expectations and cast in the mold formed by the humanistic wanderings of their own reprobate minds. Their god is absolutely and categorically foreign to the Bible.

We shall thank God for all eternity for His "marvelous grace that is greater than all our sin". Yes, and a thousand amens!! But, we must not allow ourselves to be deceived, for God will not be mocked. Not for one moment must we think that He will allow the finite mind of rebellious man to reconstruct His divine character into some spineless, indulgent deity, and His infinite purpose into some indecisive, helter-skelter proposal that is constantly up for debate. In essence God has almost been made intrinsically a human being.

The church at Laodicea was in a terrible condition. Void of any spirituality and steeped in materialism, she was the epitome of a lifeless church that was taking on the evil characteristics of the city she was supposed to influence. Little, if any difference at all, could be seen between the Christians of Laodicea and its pagan citizens.

Jesus' Advice

Repent (vs.# 19). At a point during His ministry Jesus had said, "I tell you, no, but unless you repent, you will all likewise perish." (Luke 13:3). Plain and simple, the church needed to repent. The problem, however, with repenting is that most people do not like to do this, especially publicly. You see, repenting is a very humbling experience. It is an admission of sin and a declaration of turning away from it.

The modern Laodicean church also knows nothing of repentance.   Modern religious psycho-babble says it is not a good thing because repenting can damage a person's self image and can do much harm to their psyche.   All the hype, pizzazz, programs, flashiness and noise in the world cannot keep a church alive when it has turned away from the truth, become prideful, rejected doctrine and made God into it own image.

The church at Laodicea had changed a lot from Paul's day.   It was dynamic, vibrant and effective in earlier years, but that all changed when it got too much of the world in it and not enough of it in the world.   It assumed the temperature and demeanor of her environment — and died.   DLM

Chapter 3

Is Armageddon Really the End of the World?

~ ~ ~ ~ ~

In a nutshell the world will go through the following series of events. The rapture of the church is the next event and it is imminent (1 Thessalonians chapters 1 and 4). This will be followed by a seven-year period of hell-on-earth, commonly called the tribulation, a period of time that was predicted by the prophet Daniel and described in some detail by Jesus (Daniel 9; Matthew 24). Sometime near the beginning of this period the anti-Christ will be revealed. This time of unprecedented world-wide trouble and despair will end with the second coming of Jesus to the Mount of Olives (Zechariah 14; Revelation 19; Acts 1), and the setting up of His 1000 year reign from the throne of David (Luke 1:32; Revelation 3:21; 20:4).

It is the Lord's 2nd Coming to the earth at the end of the tribulation and the resulting confrontation with Satan and his anti-Christ that is often called "The Battle of Armageddon" (Revelation 16:16). Though television programs and secular discussions virtually never go beyond that event, the truth is the world does not come to an end at Armageddon. That Armageddon ends the world is an erroneous conclusion resulting from man's tunnel-vision fascination with that battle, and his failure to study all the scriptures.

Many issues and arguments could be avoided if Bible students read all that God has said about an event, and to take His words in their contextual, simple and plain-sense meaning. Very often if there are unclear meanings regarding what God has said, it is because man has imposed upon the text a skewed template of interpretation. So, take your own Bible in hand and read for yourself God's description of Armageddon in Revelation.

Revelation 19:19-21

The assembly of the world's armies is the result of demonic influence (Revelation 16:12-16). At that point the anti-Christ (the beast) will draw a line in the sand, and will in essence demand a final confrontation with Jesus for sovereignty over the earth. Satan is infuriated that Jesus was the only One qualified to take and open the scroll (the title deed to earth; Revelation 5), and that He has poured out His wrath upon this miserable and Christ -rejecting world — the same world Satan calls his domain. His hatred for Jesus comes to its consummation as he assembles the world's armies to fight Him in Jerusalem. In preparation for what he believes will be the decisive battle of all ages, he assembles his armies in a large valley in northern Israel, the Valley of Jezreel, or Armageddon.

Contrary to entrenched human speculation, the whole thing is actually anti-climactic. The entire world shows up for a war that does not happen. There is no exchange of artillery, no maneuvers, no any such thing. Jesus, at His coming, simply speaks a word and His enemies are destroyed in a most unusual manner (Zechariah 14:12). With less effort than nonchalantly flicking a speck from His shirt sleeve, Jesus deals with Satan and his armies. The God-hating human race is due many things, and this comeuppance is just one of them that is coming.

Anti-Christ and his subservient false prophet are not killed, but are seized and thrown alive into hell. No trial, no defense, no hesitation, no anything. They are summarily dismissed to hell. Here, the most powerful mortal to have ever lived, one who had the world at his beck and call, one who dared defy God is instantly sent to eternal torment. Might we think his pride will remain as he angrily defies the fires of hell? I don't think so. Rather, I believe he will shriek in horror as he fearfully descends into heavy, thick darkness, plunging into torment and hopelessness for ever.

Those armies with the anti-Christ are killed and the ravenous birds become bloated with their corpses. Not exactly a glorious end for those who defied God, who believed in the primacy of human wisdom and capabilities and who believed there is a spark of deity in every human being. Fools, they are.

Revelation 20:1-3

Satan is laid hold of by an angel, and is thrown into the abyss, the place of the nether world where demonic spirits are imprisoned awaiting judgment. He is kept there for at least two distinct purposes. First, his imprisonment prevents him from deceiving the nations, those unsaved who survive the tribulation and go into the millennium in their mortal bodies along with those born to them. Second, his release at the end of the millennium for a short while proves something mankind has always denied. More on that shortly.

Revelation 20:4-6

Now comes the time for the glorification of those who died as martyrs during the tribulation. Quite often during the Q&A sessions after a conference on prophecy at least one person will ask if anyone will be saved during the tribulation. The answer is "yes", a great multitude will be saved (Revelation 7:9ff). They will not be members of the church, for the bride of Christ will be in His presence in heaven during those seven years. This is clear evidence that the church is not the only part of the kingdom of God. Consider also that Abraham, Isaac and Jacob and the prophets are also in the kingdom, but are not in the church (Luke 13:28).

These people will die for their faith. Put simply, they will die at the guillotine by the hand of anti-Christ. This group includes those who had not heard the gospel prior to the rapture, and perhaps those who heard but rejected it. However, there is some question about this last group. Many students believe what Paul said in 2 Thessalonians 2:7-12 might mean that those who rejected the gospel prior to the rapture will not accept it afterward. But, the most poignant truth on this matter is this: if a person rejects the gospel now when there is no real persecution in most areas, what makes that same person think they will accept it during the tribulation when the penalty will be death?

Those who accept this text literally are often accused of teaching "a second chance". That is not true. What we teach is that as long as a person is alive there is a chance, no matter the dispensation in which he lives. But, once death comes it is all over. Whatever spiritual state a person is in when he dies, he will be in that state for all eternity. Saved or lost. No gray area, no exceptions. Sobering.

What will life be like on earth at that time? Isaiah gives us just a glimpse in Isaiah 11. The interesting thing about that chapter is the description of the animal kingdom. Meat-eaters will become plant-eaters, and deadly snakes will be pets for children. This will be the earth as God intended it to be — no strife, no blood-shed, no fear, etc. What Adam and Eve lost in their rebellion in The Garden of Eden, God restores for us to enjoy just as He promised (Acts 3:21). Further more, weapons of war will no longer be needed and will be converted to implements of agriculture (Isaiah 2:4). Not since creation has the world seen this, and even then only two people have ever lived in such pristine conditions.

Revelation 20:7-10

There are several major questions that we cannot answer regarding this passage, but that does not mean we cannot draw some sound conclusions. Why would God release Satan from the abyss and allow him to deceive the nations once again? The answer to that question is implied in the text. If, after 1000 years of perfect bliss, harmony, justice and righteousness, mankind can so easily be deceived then we can conclude that sin and rebellion are not caused by a bad environment, and must be the result of something else. God says the problem is the human heart (Jeremiah 17:9). This condemnation of the human heart has no place in secular thinking, but secular thinking most often does not possess one iota of spiritual discernment. The problem is not about what is around us — it is about what is in us.

The first ones to be in hell are the anti-Christ and his false prophet, and at the end of this final rebellion Satan is thrown into the lake of fire as well. What must not be misunderstood about this verse is that there will be no comradeship in hell. The fact that other people a person might have known while on earth are also there will not bring comfort or consolation. Anything that will bring relief of any kind and to any degree will be absent, and absent for all eternity. Torment, hopelessness, memory and loneliness will fill every moment of every hour without pause or respite. And memory will haunt people in a special way. To be able to remember every neglected opportunity; to remember the faces and voices of loved ones who were saved; to remember the warnings that were scoffed at and ignored (Luke 16).

Revelation 20:11-15

Then comes the final judgment. This is the event most people have talked about for ions of time. It is vital to see that Christians are not being judged here, for their judgment for sin was the cross of Jesus (Romans 8:1). The only judgment Christians will see is the judgment seat of Christ (2 Corinthians 5:10; 1 Corinthians 3:10ff) where degrees of reward are given. It is not the same as the great white throne judgment, for even the words for "judgment" in the Revelation text and the 2 Corinthians text have totally different meanings.

The unsaved among us might not like this thought, but it remains an incontrovertible fact: their lives are incessantly moving toward this moment where every sin they have ever committed will be fully revealed. Multitudes have said for millennia they are good enough on their own to escape hell's judgment. They point to their good deeds, benevolent works, organizational membership and moral character. But, the evidence is there in the books; books with full disclosure of their lives and which are presented as irrefutable witnesses of their sin. All it takes is one sin for a person to be condemned, and instead of accepting our Lord's payment for their sin, they chose to live as they wished thinking they would be OK in their demand to meet God on this day on their own merits. Well, they do. And the verdict is guilty. No appeal.

What people generally call "the battle of Armageddon" is indeed not the end of the world, for many things must transpire before this current heavens and earth are destroyed in fervent heat (2 Peter 3:10). Actually, the Valley of Jezreel is not where the Lord will destroy His enemies; that will happen in Jerusalem (Zechariah 14:2-4). Jezreel is merely the staging point for the world's armies under the command of anti-Christ. The men will probably number in the millions, and their weapons, logistics and maintenance facilities will cover the land like vermin on a carcass. And each one will be destroyed in the same manner as those in Jerusalem.

Many people have a skewed understanding about Armageddon because they watch too much TV, while reading too little of the Bible. General of the Army Douglas MacArthur, at the surrender of the Japanese Empire on the deck of the USS Missouri on 2 September 1945, said, "If we do not now devise some greater and more equitable system, Armageddon will be at our door." The point he was making was that if the world does not find a way to avoid war in the resolution of conflict, it will be brought to destruction at Armageddon.

MacArthur was a great general, but he did not understand scripture. Not only will the world not be destroyed at Armageddon, but this battle will not be caused by some human inability to resolve conflict among nations. Satan will be behind the assembly of the world's armies to fight God.

On that day Jesus Christ will once again personally step into the affairs of this world. He will destroy every enemy and will institute His personal reign over this planet for 1000 years. He will not try to get a resolution from the U.N. allowing Him to act unilaterally. He will not concern Himself with public opinion, and He will not depend upon allies because He will have none.

Armageddon will be what is commonly called "the Second Coming". The first one had to do with stables, mangers, humility and death. The next time it will have to do with fiery judgment in righteous indignation, and the imposition of His will upon both creation and people. And, the important thing about Armageddon is it happens seven years after the rapture of the church. And that means the rapture could happen today. DLM

Chapter 4

Timothy McVeigh—He Did It His Way

~ ~ ~ ~ ~

June 11th marks the anniversary of the execution of Timothy McVeigh, the man who blew up the Alfred P. Murrah Federal Building in Oklahoma City. On April 19, 1995 McVeigh parked a truck loaded with about 1000 pounds of fertilizer mixed with fuel oil, set a fuse and left. A few minutes later 168 people were dead, including a number of children.

McVeigh was a veteran of the first Gulf War and earned a Bronze Star as a machine gunner on a Bradley Fighting Vehicle. He was an average kid in high school and showed no dangerous or disturbing traits. So, what would make an otherwise normal man do what he did?

Various people listed some issues they believed brought him to that point. His younger sister Jennifer said he was very upset at the Federal Government's handling of the Ruby Ridge and Branch Davidian standoffs.[1] McVeigh accused the government of killing innocent people including children in the blazing inferno at Waco. His sister also said he was very disappointed because he tried to join the U.S. Army's super-elite Green Beret, but was physically unable to handle the training [2].

It is evident he had a seething hatred for the government and searched for measures by which he could actively wage some kind of revolt against it. He finally chose the Murrah building because he believed the ATF agents who were responsible for the Waco fiasco had their offices there.

But, is that really what was behind his actions? Was his hatred for the government the only thing gnawing at his soul? No, probably not. His major problem could have been that he was alienated from God and was, therefore, hopeless in a world gone mad. He could see no future accountability for what he viewed as a government of injustice and fascism. That is, he saw the innocent suffering at the hands of an evil government and nobody was ever going to be held accountable.

McVeigh was raised a Catholic, but disavowed Catholicism after high school. He later became an admitted agnostic [3]. It probably was not his leaving the Catholic Church that produced such emptiness in his soul, but rather it might have been his choice to label God as some ethereal, unanswerable question.

This kind of conclusion is somewhat common among the hopeless. That is, McVeigh chose to see the totality of all life and living as being confined only to this presently polluted earth and evil world system. People like him do not understand, or believe Jesus is coming back to take His church out of the world. Further, they do not understand, or believe that same Jesus will return to this very earth, will void all forms of human government and will inaugurate a time of perfect peace and justice. It is no wonder his heart was void of hope for something better. Of course, his murderous action cannot be justified to any degree because of his empty soul.

The innocent indeed suffers, but equally true is the coming accountability for those responsible. The virtuous need not become restless and impatient, for God does not settle all accounts at the end of each day. Jesus Christ will soon hold court, and there the innocent will be vindicated and all perpetrators will be held accountable, judged and sentenced. And, it will happen in open court for all creation to witness.

McVeigh ended his life with no final words, but with a slip of paper with the William Ernest Henley poem *Invictus* written upon it. The final words of that poem are: *I am the Master of my fate; I am the Captain of my soul.* It seems he was trying to make a poignant statement in death that everybody would remember. The truth, though, is both Henley and McVeigh were wrong — oh, so wrong!! We are not masters and captains of anything, and to think we are is to be foolish; fools duped by the lie that we can somehow be renown by doing whatever we want, in the way we want, outside the will of God and without accountability.

Remember the words of the Apostle Paul: *Do not be deceived, God is not mocked; for whatever a man sows, this he will also reap* (Galatians 6:7 NASB). Actually, the only real control we have in our lives is in deciding to follow Jesus Christ or not. Everything else is just consequences.

End notes:
1) Jennifer McVeigh calmly describes her brother's hatred. Online www.cnn.com/
        US/9705/mcveigh.late/. Cited 18 May 05
2) McVeigh letters to family are portrait of anger and alienation. Online
        www.marijuananews.com/marijuananews/cowan/timo
        thy_mcveigh_letters_to_Family.htm. Cited 18 May 05
3) McVeigh took last rites before execution. Online
        www.cnn.law.printthis.clickability.com/pt/cpt?
        acion=cpt&expire=1&urlID=11992008&fb= Y&rul=http%3A%2F%
2Farchives.cnn.com%2F. Cited 18 May 05

Chapter 5

The Measure of National Greatness

~ ~ ~ ~ ~

It is true that one of the last bastions of the biblical world view of life is the United States, but she is in dire trouble, crumbling fast into the dust pile of once-great nations. Some people will take issue with that statement, but their defense is mostly built upon emotion that has little semblance to reality. No American relishes this thought, and for some of us it is so hateful it is difficult to even think about. Yet, if the moral health of our country were put on a graft the line would show a definite downturn, perhaps even a free-fall in the last few years.

Any number of questions might be asked regarding the situation, such as how is this moral dereliction happening, why is it happening and what is the answer? Most such questions are open-ended which means there is no end to opinions that might be offered. Still, an objective examination will reveal a disturbing fact about our national life — we're dying spiritually. That does not mean we have no religion in America; it means it has little to do with God.

Presently some political candidates, talk-show hosts and other celebrities along with any number of other people are touting our national greatness. There is no question whatsoever that our country is great in many ways with the invention, production and distribution of goods and services that are nothing less than indispensable for the comfort and welfare of not only our own citizens, but many the world over. Our national benevolence is unprecedented. There is no tragedy anywhere on this planet that does not see the immediate and wholesale response of our country with food, water, clothing, fuel, temporary housing, medicine and anything else we have that might be needed — all free!

One could add to that all our efforts to protect and provide for the weak and needy of the world through numerous treaties that have cost us so much in both blood and money. If Europe and Asia were to repay our country for their blood-bought freedom, provision and resulting affluence our national debt would be seriously curved and there would be no threat to our dollar remaining the world's reserve currency. And, you can add to that everything we have done for Africa, South America, the Caribbean, etc. Further, such debts to our country are often forgiven by us, and unfortunately, forgotten about by those who benefitted from our generosity.

And, all this benevolence is happening in spite of the fact the value of our dollar is dropping like a rock. Further, many American jobs are now being done by enemy nations sorely hostile toward us; nations that export their mostly cheap products to us in mega-volumes are being sold in our nation's largest retail stores. Just try to find a jacket, drill bit, radio, etc., for sale in just about any American store that is not made by those who would destroy us...and the list could go on.

All of this is to say that our country is not without greatness and benevolence. It cannot be denied.

Try, however, to look at this at another, and perhaps deeper level. Try to see us as God sees us. Try to imagine what really makes a country and her people great. Is it wealth and benevolence? To be sure, at least to some degree, but is that all? Might there be something of greater value than those things?

There is. And, it has to do with the spirit and soul of a nation's people.

By God's standard generosity is trumped by godliness. The cliché is true that a person can be generous without being godly, but cannot be godly without being generous. Yet, the crux of it all goes far deeper than a simple cliché. Along with Madison Avenue's full-color portrayals of our affluence and television news pictures of our charity, there are other indicators that show a far different picture. To the heart that is sensitive to the biblical worldview those indicators are dark and vile; heavy with foreboding and impending judgment.

The evidence is clear that our country is immersed into a culture that is lower than that of simple lasciviousness. Immorality is no longer the descriptive term; amorality is a better word. From what is displayed in film, music, literature and television it is evident our culture is no longer ashamed of shacking up, illegitimate children, homosexuality, public nudity, gutter-filth profanity, etc. When you add violence in the form of murder, mayhem, rape, abortion, robbery and intimidation there can be no doubt as to the extent of our degradation.

When middle-school girls take pictures of themselves in the nude and send them to boys as sort of an adolescent matchmaking service something is wrong. Those kids have probably never blushed even once in their lives. The question is not where did they learn this, but how did they come to view this as something they would even consider doing?! Scandalous pictures of nationally known beauty-pageant winners are distributed on the web for multitudes to see. And, there is no shame.

Spring break on our nation's beaches is the scene of antics that seemingly set new precedents for low-life conduct each year. As portrayed in some news reports the revelers function as catalysts among themselves producing infectious lewd behavior that quickly escalates and spreads to become the norm. Nothing is hidden or withheld. And, there is no shame.

That their conduct might very well be displayed on the web, that it might be seen by their parents and grandparents, that their future spouses and children might see it, that it might destroy future opportunities are of no concern whatsoever. In short they willingly act with the morals of mongrel dogs with no remorse at all. And, there is no shame.

The executive, legislative and judicial branches of our great nation are tainted and fouled by adulterous behavior, homosexual and lesbian perversion, corruption and every sewer-bottom level of life one might imagine. The national inclination in education is to dispense with science and accept the ridiculous theory of evolution that decrees we came from a slime pit, there is no God, no heaven, no hell and no accountability. There are no longer any absolutes by which we might live; everything is relative to the moment. It is not about what is inherently right or wrong, but how one might feel about it. Feelings, emotions and intentions have replaced the indisputable.

It is now religiously fashionable to say everybody is going to heaven. Nobody may offend the heathen by saying the Bible is the sole and final authority on the subject. Oprah Winfrey, proud advocate of 21st century new ageism and who says Jesus is just one of many ways to eternal bliss, is now God in the minds of some of her followers. And, for heaven's sake we must not be judgmental of those who follow paganism in any of its sordid forms because everybody is right and nobody is wrong. Toleration, you see, is the key.

Yes, America seems to be the last refuge for the faithful practice of Christianity, but that is rapidly changing. How long before an American preacher will be arrested, prosecuted, sentenced and imprisoned for a lengthy term under some so-called hate-crimes statute because he quoted the Bible regarding sexual promiscuity and perversion? Soon, perhaps? How long before the government, by bureaucratic or judicial fiat, removes what has always been the sacred right of parents to oversee the education of their children and to teach them the biblical view? We are presently seeing the foundation for that with the politically liberal push for US ratification of the UN Convention on the Rights of the Child.

It is true there is still a remnant in our country that has not capitulated, but that group is growing smaller, is having less national influence and is living under progressively more stringent opposition.

When you get to the analysis of all this, however, an interesting question begins to develop. At what point will God finally get enough and drop the shoe of punishment? Perhaps when God makes His move it might come in the form of something of more consequence than mere punishment; it might be in the form of a judgment as was the case with the world in Noah's day, or Sodom, or the Egyptian Pharaoh, or the Amorites. Will it come in the distant future? Is it imminent? Or, maybe we might ask if it is past due? No one can say, but it should be very clear to every Christian that God does have a limit and that He is no respecter of persons or nations when it comes to dealing with blatant amorality and the in-your-face attitude many have toward Him.

Benevolence, even sacrificial benevolence, can in no way even approach the point where it can equate to, or substitute for righteousness. Not that the secular aspect of America is attempting such an agreement with God (for they could not care less what God thinks), but this should serve to wake up the "Christian" segment of America to the fact that God is not impressed with our good deeds, national or personal. If that were the case then His sending Jesus as the sole sacrifice for our sin was a terrible mistake. Perish the thought!

What is the answer? Many things could be said, but space will not allow it. So, perhaps we might take a cue from the actions of President Abraham Lincoln and the US Senate in the 1860s. Lincoln's "Day of National Humiliation, Fasting and Prayer" is reprinted for your consideration. Would any modern, sitting president follow suit? Don't look for that to happen, though, because I do not believe any modern president, or U.S. Senate body has the spiritual depth and the political will necessary to do it. And further, it seems abundantly clear those wishing to become president also fall short.

The eternal truth is that God will not be mocked by any nation or person. What is planted is what is harvested. DLM

By the President of the United States of America.

A Proclamation.

Whereas, the Senate of the United States, devoutly recognizing the Supreme Authority and just Government of Almighty God, in all the affairs of men and of nations, has, by a resolution, requested the President to designate and set apart a day for National prayer and humiliation.

And whereas it is the duty of nations as well as of men, to own their dependence upon the overruling power of God, to confess their sins and transgressions, in humble sorrow, yet with assured hope that genuine repentance will lead to mercy and pardon; and to recognize the sublime truth, announced in the Holy Scriptures and proven by all history, that those nations only are blessed whose God is the Lord.

And, insomuch as we know that, by His divine law, nations like individuals are subjected to punishments and chastisements in this world, may we not justly fear that the awful calamity of civil war, which now desolates the land, may be but a punishment, inflicted upon us, for our presumptuous sins, to the needful end of our national reformation as a whole People? We have been the recipients of the choicest bounties of Heaven. We have been preserved, these many years, in peace and prosperity. We have grown in numbers, wealth and power as no other nation has ever grown. But we have forgotten God. We have forgotten the gracious hand which preserved us in peace, and multiplied and enriched and strengthened us; and we have vainly imagined, in the deceitfulness of our hearts, that all these blessings were produced by some superior wisdom and virtue of our own. Intoxicated with unbroken success, we have become too self-sufficient to feel the necessity of redeeming and preserving grace, too proud to pray to the God that made us!

It behooves us then, to humble ourselves before the offended Power, to confess our national sins, and to pray for clemency and forgiveness.

Chapter 6

The New Decade

~ ~ ~ ~ ~

No man, Bible prophecy teacher or not, can specifically predict what will happen in the future. But, we have not been left in the dark about what is on the near horizon. We can make some fairly good guesses by noting the past, seeing where we are presently and putting it all in perspective with the template of Bible prophecy. And, the key to getting the clearest picture possible is the avoidance of both sensationalism and secular bias, for the former skews the truth and the latter denies it. Said another way, to see what is coming simply examine what God has said then look at what is happening before your very eyes.

The world is falling down around us with no hope in sight from the secular viewpoint. Yet, this fact is denied daily by those who believe in the power and determination of the human race. They portray their secular hopes in movies, TV sitcoms, newspaper op-eds and by any other means possible. The mantra goes something like this: *Yes, things are bad, but they've been bad before. And, just as we've solved serious problems before, we will do it again. All we need to do is to come together, pool our resources, choose a real leader, get rid of nationalism and borders, restrict personal liberty for the good of the planet, focus on the godhood that is in all of us and we will most certainly overcome.* This is the kind of claptrap that comes from other politicians and cultured secularists who are clueless about what God has said.

Consider several things that might be on the future's short list.

Increasing trend toward Globalism

Globalism is officially defined as an international geopolitical policy in which the entire world is regarded as the appropriate sphere for any state's influence. In plain language it means the world becomes a single state. To add more clarity I would add that it emphasizes the centralization of political, economic and military power along with a singular, inclusive religion. The European Union is a good example of evolving globalism in that EU member states have essentially given up sovereignty in order to be part of it.

The United States is more deeply involved in the globalist effort than many might think. This is seen in many ways, not the least of which is found in our judicial system. Any number of judges, including some members of the U.S. Supreme Court, advocates taking foreign law into consideration when establishing legal precedent.

The effort toward globalizing the planet is not limited to economics and politics, but includes religion and its critical building block, the family. Globalists understand they must necessarily destroy the very foundation of biblical order, a foundation that manifests itself in the family.

For this reason we might expect continued pressure on the U.S. Senate to ratify the UN Convention on the Rights of the Child. This global directive has been ratified by every member of the UN except Somalia and the United States, and Somalia has said they will ratify it. All signatories are required to "act in the best interest of the child", with the world-state deciding what is best.

Basically, the eventual result will be American legal sovereign-

The New Decade 43

ty being trumped, and especially the rights of parents. Is the
United States ready for world bureaucrats to dictate to parents
how to raise their children? Regrettably, many elected leaders
believe so.

Globalization will produce a legal system wherein parents who
teach their children the biblical worldview will be charged with
child abuse, or reckless endangerment, or some other indictment
requiring state custody of their children.

Growing Islamic Influence and Belligerence

On the Temple Mount in Jerusalem there are water faucets
where Moslems wash their feet before going into the mosques
to pray to Allah. America, however, does not provide public
foot-washing faucets. So, at the Indianapolis airport in 2007
Moslem taxi drivers decided to wash their feet in the sinks in
the traveler's restrooms before praying, something found to be
disgusting to travelers. Since political correctness requires
Moslems be appeased at any cost to everybody else, the new
addition to the airport buildings included floor-level sinks for
the dirty feet.

Moslems in some areas of America want to be governed by Islamic sharia law instead of American law. The thing about Islamic law is it is not merely part of their religion, it is the basis
for life; a 7th century pagan lifestyle to be exact. What most
people do not understand is Islam is not simply about going to a
mosque, but it is about what you eat, what school you attend,
how you dress, who you hate, how many wives a man has, etc.

And, Moslems are now being welcomed into our government.
President Barack Hussein Obama has appointed two Moslems
to very important and sensitive positions in the U.S. government. Arif Alikhan is now Assistant Secretary for Policy Development at the Dept. of Homeland Security, and Kareem
Shora (born in Syria) is now a member of the Homeland Security Advisory Council. Both are referred to by the Obama admin-

istration as "devout Moslems".

In the same vein, watch for Iran to increase her animosity toward all things Christian and Jewish. The threats from the ayatollahs and Ahmadinejad will not likely go away. Especially as they near the completion of an atomic weapon and its delivery system.

Ongoing dilution of Christianity

Christian sectarianism based upon opinion is unbiblical (Romans 14). Equally true is the fact that taking a strong stand for scriptural truth is biblical (Jude 3, 4). Yet, modern religionists do not agree that standing for biblical truth is good, for they seem to really enjoy their pompous smiles and pursed lips as they label "fundamentalists" as unsophisticated religious morons. Religious inclusiveness will persist in being the new god of the religiously sophisticated crowd, and it will continue to happen in direct proportion to the dilution of biblical truth.

Sadly, many of those people are at least somewhat biblically literate. That is, many were biblically sound at some point in their lives. Though they know the truth, yet they place themselves in the inclusive crowd for social and business reasons, justifying it all by pointing to what they call narrow-minded parents, and closed-minded churches. Truth becomes no longer important as long as they are lauded and labeled as "progressive" by modern emergent church leaders and friends.

The result is two-fold: First, people will go where they will hear what they want to hear about themselves. And, they do not want to hear anything from the pulpit about sin, righteousness and coming judgment because those subjects are too passé and uninspiring, you see. Second, the shell of the modern church appears clean and polished from the outside, but the inside is putrefied with spiritual rot as seen by the growing attitude that God is no longer to be honored and respected, but rather He becomes everybody's home-boy/good-buddy. Add to that, if you will, a cavalier, if not down-right militant, opinion regarding prophecy. The slope becomes so slippery that the truth is soon unrecognizable. Quickly, the slide becomes so steep and the ride becomes so exhilarating that people do not see the destructive end.

Harassment of Christians

It is not only coming, it is here! In Santa Rosa County, California "communication with a deity" is prohibited, school officials cannot bow their heads if someone else is praying and they cannot reply to any email that contains religious language. Nurse Catherina Cenzon-DeCarlo has sued Mt. Sinai Hospital for forcing her to participate in an abortion, or face disciplinary action. Toni Lemly won her court case in Louisiana when she was fired for refusing to administer the "morning after pill". A Christian photographer in New Mexico was found guilty of discrimination when he refused to photograph a homosexual "wedding". Julea Ward is suing Eastern Michigan University because they dismissed her from a counseling program because she refused to affirm homosexual behavior. (All cases cited above are from World, 16 January 2010, p. 48).

Expect such cases to increase in number. Christians are going to be stripped of their "right of conscience" at every opportunity. And, in the near future this will not only apply to public jobs and private enterprise as we understand those terms, but we can look for freedom of conscience to be attacked should a member of the U.S. military refuse to take part in future martial -law operations against what Homeland Security Secretary Janet Napolitano calls those right-wing, religious, military-veterans who are against homosexual rights and abortion.

Think it can't happen? History students remember Union General Benjamin "The Beast" Butler and his infamous Order # 28 for women in New Orleans in 1862. It stated, *Any woman who might By word, gesture, or movement show contempt for any officer or soldier could be used as a Woman of the town plying her vocation.*" That is, could be used as a prostitute. In essence rape was legalized under martial law. Further, it was not just the suspension of civil liberty that was so egregious, but the vindictive, in-your-face attitude of the U.S. government.

The use of the military in civilian law enforcement duties is prohibited by the "Posse Comitatus Act" (Latin: force, or power, of the county). However, this prohibition is suspended during times of insurrection or national disaster. Hence when a U.S. president declares martial-law a number of constitutional liberties are ignored. The logical question is what defines insurrection or national disaster? The answer is it depends on who is president and what is his agenda. You see how far this can go. You might wish to read the *John Warner National Defense Authorization Act* which went into effect 17 October 2006, particularly Section 1076 regarding use of the Armed Forces during emergencies.

What do you suppose will happen when an U.S. Army MP platoon shows up at someone's home or church with orders to arrest and detain a private citizen for speaking out against the government during an incident some president has declared as a "public insurrection or national disaster"? It is not easy to think about it, but it appears these matters are presently being discussed at numerous coffee klatches and other gatherings. As one national reporter said last year, such fear and distrust of government has not been seen since 1860.

And, this kind of distrust is not owned solely by Americans, but essentially by the whole world. What is happening in America has already happened in Europe, Asia, Russia, South America, etc. The careful observer will see something coming together on a worldwide scale that is unprecedented. Further, that "something" is not so much a visible plan-by-the-numbers, but more of an ebbing and flowing process that has no definite form, at least at this point. Yet, like a shapeless flow of lava, it slowly, but surely captures and consumes all resistance. The result of this process will be chaos and fear, and will thus solidify to become the stage upon which anti-Christ will appear. He will appease the masses, and replace chaos and fear with stability. And, by that time the world will be so tired of terror and turmoil it will welcome him with open arms and at any cost.

Is the world re-living the 1930s? Though not entirely the same, yet there are some parallels. In 1938 Mao Zedong, the late and bloody Chinese Communist dictator, said, "Political power grows out of the barrel of a gun." Adolf Hitler had the same philosophy. His SS and Gestapo henchmen were fond of saying to those who opposed Nazism based upon the rule of German law: "You have your law and I have my gun. Who do you think will win?"

So, what is the bottom line? Things will not get any better. The U.S. Constitution cannot hold back a demonically inspired agenda when it has the backing of powerful political figures.

But, do not fear. God told us it would be this way. As we race toward socialism and totalitarianism (national and international) we fight those battles we can, but our real hope is not in human government because even the best is tainted. Actually, our hope is in the imminent rapture of the church. And regarding the liberty-robbing agendas of puny human demagogues, do not worry — Jesus will not only pour out His wrath on their fiefdoms for seven years, but during the ensuing millennium He will smash every dictator-want-to-be into submission and make them like it. Thank God there is more to the kind of life we were created by God to live than what can be found on this present earth.

And, those around us need to hear this message of hope. They do not know the truth, and thus live in fear and anxiety. What a joy it is to see despair become hope in the lives of those who were formerly called "earth dwellers". DLM

Chapter 7

The Events of Revelation 13

~ ~ ~ ~ ~

This chapter is one of the most interesting in the book of Revelation because it gives us a broad look at the work of anti-Christ and his worldwide administration during the tribulation period. As a preface, it is important to understand nobody today knows who this man might be. Many names have been offered, but the truth is they are all speculative. Some will try to speak definitively on their proposed candidate for the office, but God has quite simply chosen to not reveal his identity. We are correct in saying his nationality will be that of a country that was part of the old Roman Empire (Daniel 9:26), and that he will come from the "sea", a term that means the mass of humanity (Revelation 17:15). This is important because it clarifies his being a human and not some demonic spirit made incarnate.

After the rapture it will become easy for his identity to be revealed. In those tumultuous days immediately after the rapture there might be any number of men jockeying for recognition and clamoring for the world's attention, but only one will be elevated above all others and he will be Satan's man (Revelation 13:2). It probably won't take very long for his dominance to be asserted and all competition to be eliminated. His identity will be positively revealed when he brokers a treaty with Israel (Daniel 9:27). The term "the many" might be a statement whose purpose is to contrast the large number of Jews in Israel at that time with "the few" that will remain at the end of the tribulation after anti-Christ kills millions of them.

We are not told everything about this treaty, but in light of Middle East politics just prior to the rapture it seems quite reasonable it will have to do with several issues critical to Israel and even to her Arab neighbors. It is possible this deal will include the right of the Jews to rebuild their Temple on the Temple Mt., something presently impossible due to the virulent hatred Moslems have for Jews. Further, the Russia/Iran threat might also be a variable in this agreement, for this coalition will come against Israel for the express purpose of destroying her. Some place this event (Ezekiel 38 & 39) prior to the rapture. That could happen, but I believe the fulfillment will be post-rapture for two reasons. First, to have it pre-rapture is to deny the imminent rapture of the church because the Russia/Iran confederation is not established to such a degree at the moment. It is moving in that direction very rapidly, but until now the actors have not taken their final places on the stage for that particular scene to be played out. Second, the miraculous destruction of this confederation will open the way for anti-Christ to move from benevolent leader of the world to tyrannical dictator of the world with no serious threat from any of the world's major players.

At some point in the process anti-Christ will suffer a fatal wound, probably to the head. His miraculous recovery will cause the entire world to stand in awe of him and to willingly offer their worship. Of all the ingredients found in this receipt for a one-world government, this should be the least surprising because it is not uncommon for masses of people to willingly bow down to a mortal they believe has all the answers to all their problems.

Some might remember Paul Henri Spaak, the former Prime Minister of Belgium and the European Parliament's first president, who said, *"We do not want another committee. We have too many already. What we want is a man of sufficient stature to hold the allegiance of all people, and to lift us out of the economic morass in which we are sinking. Send us such a man and, be he God or the devil, we will receive him."* At a precise moment such a man will present himself to the world as its savior, and humanity will say with great relief, "Finally…!" Little will the world know exactly what it has so willingly accepted.

Not only will anti-Christ turn against Israel with a vengeance, but he will "make war with the saints and…overcome them." Who are those saints? Well, first of all everybody who is a disciple of Jesus Christ is a saint. The word simply means "holy ones". Those saints who will die in the tribulation are not Christians as we commonly understand the term today, for the church will be gone at this point. But, they are saints anyway, and in the sense that the term "Christian" simply means a follower of Christ, they can also be called Christians. There were saints during the Old Testament era prior to Pentecost, and there will be saints in the post-rapture period, too. These will be people who know the truth and refuse to worship the anti-Christ or take his mark. Most will have to die for their faith, and are seen in Revelation 7:14 and 20:4.

Interestingly another beast arises, but this time from "the earth" instead of "the sea". It is difficult to determine what that term might mean. A thorough study of 1 Samuel 28:13 and Psalm 10:18 might shed some light on it. This false prophet is also a man and not a demon spirit, and will do nine things as listed from verse 12 to verse 17.

It is possible this false prophet will come from, or least have roots in, any one of several modern churches; churches commonly characterized by two major features: liturgy and control. The description God gives in Revelation 17:1-4 shows a church steeped in pomp, wealth, form, fashion and protocol. It is visible and impressive, but cold, empty and void of the Holy Spirit. It is mystic and sensual, and as such becomes a great tool in the hands of anti-Christ.

The leader of this harlot church and his clerical minions will have no qualms whatsoever about forcing every human to bow before anti-Christ in worship. In like manner they will have no qualms about cutting off the heads of every one who refuses to do so. Simple as that. The Spanish Inquisition is a precedent for using torture and murder as incentive.

How will the false prophet enforce such control over people? He will do it with a visible mark of some kind. No body knows what the mark will be, but it will have something to do with the number 666. The technology for this kind of control and accounting is available today, and when the time comes it will simply be suited to accommodate his demands.

It must be emphasized that today the number 666 means absolutely nothing relative to anti-Christ. Some people refuse to have 666 as house numbers, license plate numbers, account numbers or other numbers associated with their identity because they think it is the "mark of the beast". Rest at ease, for 666 is NOT the "mark of the beast" today. Such mark will not come into existence prior to the rapture. Secular society already has enough ammunition to use in its indictment that Christians are stupid and superstitious. We do not need to give them more by being so concerned about something that is presently a non-issue. Fear and ignorance breeds this kind of overreaction — like a hotel not having a 13th floor!

To not be able to buy or sell without the mark will be a death stroke in many ways, yet some recklessly believe they will be able to escape the wrath and control of anti-Christ by living in secluded wilderness areas. Space will not allow the listing of all the reasons why this is such foolish thinking, but one thing must be considered. Children will be born during this period, and without the mark parents will not be able to get treatment and medication for a sick child. In essence the choice will be taking the mark or allowing the child to die. For those who know the truth about the consequence of taking the mark this will be a choice that is horrible beyond imagination. In the end, though, everyone will take it or die.

The current worldwide emphasis on the worship of the Divine Feminine (the apparition appearing in various places today) among Catholics, Moslems, Hindus, any number of Protestants and others will play a significant role in the work of this false prophet. The key will be deception. If a person at that time, or any other time for that matter, does not know the truth, that person is a candidate for believing the lie as Eve did in the Garden, and as multitudes of her progeny have since then.

Much could be written about the events of Revelation and chapter 13 specifically. But, more important than reading what someone else has written on the subject, it is our responsibility to read it for ourselves. These things were not dictated by Jesus and written by John just to gather dust on some shelf or table. Knowing the truth will increase one's faith and will erase fear and joy-robbing apprehension that comes from ignorance. DLM

For God has not destined us for wrath, but for obtaining salvation through our Lord Jesus Christ...1Thess 5:9

Chapter 8

Earth Day

~ ~ ~ ~ ~

The whole world is again celebrating "mother earth" in honor of Earth Day. Even Google™ has gotten in on the action by coloring their logo green. Politicians are making "green" speeches, and corporations are donating millions to groups emphasizing the dire consequences of global warming. This seems to be the number one mantra for the 21st century environmentalists.

As Christians no one should be more sensitive to proper stewardship of the earth and terrestrial resources, but we must never elevate this speck of cosmic dust to the level of deity, as some have done. Not only that, but some of those people become visibly upset and become violent and destructive if the rest of us do not subscribe, at least to some level of allegiance, to their god. Green has become the primary color for the disciples of environmentalism, and they rally around trees singing their hymns of adoration to the creature instead of the Creator.

And that is the problem. Yes, sensible use of resources and genuine husbandry of what God has given us to sustain and enhance life is not only responsible conduct, but is expected of us by our Creator. However, mankind's undue emphasis upon this physical world system is horribly misplaced. This world is destined for fiery destruction, not at the hand of man, but at the hand of God (2 Peter 3:10-13). Though that same text clearly says that the object of our focus is not a "what", but the "Who", yet many people reject that great truth.

It would be very wise to closely monitor what you are accepting regarding Earth Day and all the rest that goes along with it. Further, it would be very wise to clarify all this for your children, for if you leave their thinking to what they get in the majority of government schools they will very soon have a skewed view of stewardship. Such as...

— Julianne Skai Arbor, an artist from Santa Rosa, was selling nude pictures of herself posing with trees for $4 each.*

—"I consider it splendid," said a beaming Bill Trampleasure, a retired Berkeley mailman who was handing out Barack Obama leaflets and greeting old friends. "I'm pushing Obama. I'm pushing the United Nations. I'm pushing Earth Day. It's all connected. I'm an old Berkeleyan - this is a great day."*

*From SFGate cited 22 April 08

Chapter 9

Getting Easier to Let Go

~ ~ ~ ~ ~

Admittedly we have it good in our country, and there is certainly nothing unholy about enjoying the blessings God has given us. However, because we are inherently so earthly-oriented it becomes difficult at times to think about the fact that we are only here temporarily. With our affluence, good health and here-to-fore bright prospects for our material futures, we tend to give most of our attention to this life, and precious little thought to the life to come. For some of us, the only thing that will cause us to refocus our attention is to become uncomfortable with the here and now. Seriously uncomfortable. And, from where I sit it looks like our comfort level is rapidly deteriorating.

Christians who suffer terminal ailments and dread diseases are often not so easily distracted from spiritual matters by the pursuit of "the good times". They are constantly made to face suffering and the brevity of life itself. Those hurting among us soon learn to not put much trust in the sick-care professions, their investment portfolios and national politics for anything of real substance. These folks tend to seriously think about matters of eternity because they understand the bonds that tether them to this life are very fragile and are soon to be broken.

But, the matter of physical health is not the point of this article.

There is something else that is emerging that makes it increasingly easy for all believers to lessen their grip on this world. In short, I believe God is allowing evil to increase to such a level of moral and spiritual pollution that God's people — no matter how comfortable they might be — are becoming increasingly aware that this world is indeed not their real home. Further, God's people, or at least some of them, are becoming disappointed and disillusioned even with those things they have historically clung to and have always considered as worthy of support and admiration. Things such as those traditional bastions of national pride that have simply lost their seemingly indomitable credibility.

For American Christians to begin to see that their country is in the toilet politically, economically and morally is very disappointing, especially for those old enough to remember how much better things used to be. In the past students could pray and read the Bible in public school. Taxes were much lower; that is, not only was the rate lower, but we were taxed on fewer things. Children could actually inherit family farms and businesses without having to sell out in order to pay inheritance and capital gains taxes. No body brought a weapon to school to harm anybody. Sexual perversion was openly declared as being evil. Promiscuity was frowned upon. Agreements were concluded with a word and a handshake. Everybody could connect with Norman Rockwell and his "Americana". Those days, however, are not simply gone, but gone forever.

But, there is something else involved here, and this is where it gets very uncomfortable for many of us. We are so patriotically oriented that admitting to the escalating demise of our once-great republic seems like something akin to treason. Criticism of our national institutions because they no longer undergird the historical interpretation of the Constitution and our traditional way of living is not easy, yet we are forced to admit it is happening.

We proudly stand and salute the American flag at Friday night ball games, after a full week of seeing that same flag fly over a government that defiantly ignores the will of tax-paying citizens. We sacrifice our warrior's blood in order to cast our votes, yet we detest the elected political hogs that belly-up to the taxpayer's trough. We honor our military, but at the same time we have a growing revulsion toward the shedding of American blood for countries that flat-out hate us. As a result many people are drawing bolder lines of distinction between government and country in an effort to live with the contradictions that can no longer be denied.

But, even this kind of rationalization is not enough to ease our doubting consciences and extinguish the flames of growing unrest with what we see happening. We now face the fact that the deep emotional ties we have to this world and especially to our country no longer have the strength they used to have. For some of us, this is what it takes to let go.

Emotional ties play important roles in many things such as those good-natured rivalries among the branches of the Armed Forces, and the competition between college and professional athletic teams from a person's alma mater or home-town. So, it is quite natural for people to love their native countries and those ties that bind them together.

We must admit that America is unique among nations, and we are very thankful to God for this. Our American republic has been a haven for multitudes for a long time, and the simple presence of an American Embassy or Consulate is a very comforting thing if a citizen is in trouble in a foreign country, especially if that country is Moslem or Communist. Yet, honesty forces us to admit America is in a tightening spiral that will obviously end in destruction. And, contrary to what politicians say there is no hope.

Bible prophecy is clear. No nation is exempt from the rapidly approaching judgment of God. No, not one. Nor is any nation exempt from the consequences of its foolish pursuit of insanity in the guise of political correctness.

Officially Sanctioned Dismissal of God

The enemies of God in America are hiding behind the cloak of "separation of church and state". Though that phrase is not used in the U.S. Constitution, and though our Founding Fathers never intended for God to be dismissed from affairs of State, yet secularists incessantly repeat the mantra in their efforts to get rid of every vestige of God, and they have been exceptionally successful. The Constitution guarantees our citizens the right to publicly practice their religion, but secularists are diligently working to force biblical Christianity into some ambiguous and impotent realm of absolute anonymity. Strange, though, and it seems almost by design that other religions are not infringed upon, whether Islam, secularism, New Age, atheism, etc.

The word "God", it seems, is to eventually be erased from coinage, oaths, official methods of dating events, official seals, etc. So strong and visceral is their hatred of God that He is to become totally obsolete and forgotten. Admitting this is not easy for us, but the fact cannot be ignored. The connection between America and our Creator, who endowed us with certain unalienable rights, no longer has the power and assurance it once had.

Destruction of American Military Effectiveness

Most every veteran I know is almost constantly at a flash-point when it comes to defending the honor of our Armed Forces. We are not to be trifled with regarding the United States military. But — and this cannot be denied — things are not like they used to be. Most veterans would have extreme difficulty serving today. And, not because we had to do PT in fatigues and combat boots while the troops today have gym shorts and running shoes. There are other things that are weakening our connection with an institution we once thought inviolate.

The repeal of "don't ask, don't tell" regarding homosexuals in the Armed Forces is the lowest point in our nation's military history. Politically correct and politically motivated admirals and general officers have no qualms about opening the door to homosexuals. Seems they cannot remember how important discipline is on a perimeter. Their actions indicate they have no experience in the conduct of tactical battle planning, offensive or defensive, or they have forgotten some important things they have learned. Probably the truth is they simply do not care as long as they get promoted to some rank that has at least one star. Those officers and senior NCOs who resist this madness because of just plain common sense, or because of a biblical worldview are most likely counseled to retire.

The weakening of America's military is also seen in the integration of men and women in some very dangerous situations. Placing a man and woman alone for hours on end in the depths of a missile silo, or on a perimeter listening post, or in any such environment is a very great risk. It is a risk to vigilance and success in warfare, not to mention a risk to whatever families that might be represented in such circumstances. Those situations which would not have even been considered before are now offered wholesale in spite of the great potential for concession, loss and destruction.

In the 1980s a feminist activist said such sexual dalliances would seldom, if ever, happen because members of the Armed Forces are professionals. They are, but, as someone else answered: secular human sexual behavior will trump professionalism most anywhere most every time; it happens in state executive mansions and in the White House. It also happens regularly in military barracks. Are the American people so foolish as to believe it would not happen in the confines of a remote, critical area?

For many Americans the effectiveness of our republic's Armed Forces is the last hope for sustained liberty, and this lends to a very strong emotional tie that historically has been strenuously defended. But, when that bond is compromised in the face of irrefutable facts the result is a forlorn sense of, "Well, what is the use anymore?"

Government Nannyship

If social engineers have their way children born in our country today will be unduly influenced by the public school system, which is an extension of government. Parents are presently having fewer choices in what their kids will eat, drink, wear, possess, etc. Bureaucrats actually believe they know more about raising kids than parents, and there is no end to their methods and degrees of interference. The bond between public schools and Christian parents has been stretched to the breaking point. The neighborhood school concept is now extinct, and this has caused many parents to completely sever all ties and resort to other means of educating their children.

God is very clear in His plan for raising children...that is the job of parents. True, in cases of abuse steps must be taken to protect children. The growing problem, however, is secular government paints the definition of abuse with a very wide brush. This, it seems, is part of the groundwork for the fulfillment of Matthew 10:16-23. That prophecy goes far beyond the work of the twelve disciples by reaching into the distant future when the believing remnant of the Jews will be preaching the gospel during the tribulation prior to Jesus' second coming. Note especially vs# 21..."And brother will deliver up brother to death, and a father his child; and children will rise up against parents, and cause them to be put to death." (NASB). We are living in the dark shadow of that kind of society this very day.

Dangerous Doctrine

There are also things of a religious nature that are making it easy for Christians to let go of this world. At least for those who study for themselves and do not accept carte-blanche everything some religious leader tells them. The teaching of the "name it and claim it" doctrine is just one of many. Sunday morning religious programming is filled with charlatans telling gullible audiences that God wants everybody to be rich and healthy, and if you are not then your faith is lacking. And, we can add to the list of attacks on truth the rejection of such doctrines as the depravity of the human heart, the necessity of the blood-atonement, salvation by grace and not by works, the resurrection of Jesus, and the increasing vitriol toward the doctrines of the rapture of the church and Jesus' post tribulation second coming.

With all that, and much more, there is no wonder that some Christians are finding it easier to deemphasize earthly mortality and to care less about those bonds that tie us to this world. Those few understand that to have the money of Carlos Helu', Bill Gates and Warren Buffet combined means nothing, and especially so if they lose their souls in the process (Matthew 16:26).

These are matters of great importance, and most any discussion about them produces a lot of questions, some of which can become very emotional. But, perhaps the deeper questions are, Why would any Christian among us wish to maintain undue ties with a world that is on a collision course with destruction, and a government that proposes to dismiss God and His word, destroy the Divine-order of the home all while simultaneously denigrating His people? Just what is it about this life that makes Christians long for earthly things that can never satisfy when God has guaranteed us a level of life that the human mind quite simply cannot imagine (1 Corinthians 2:9)?

At least part of the answer is we are spiritually fallen human beings endued with the Adamic nature. And, this brings us to somewhat of a frightful reality; that no one among us is immune from holding too tightly to this world. In the 2000 years of church history it has never been more important than today for God's people to tune in to current events and to examine them in light of Bible prophecy. Study Bible prophecy — God did not put it into the Bible as a second-tier space-filler!

These matters are not easy to address. But, they must be addressed in order for us to clearly and unemotionally face reality. Are we seriously uncomfortable yet? If not, what do you think God will have to do to get us to that point?

It is true that though we are still allowed as free people to fight tyranny, yet as citizens of this republic we have certain obligations that God expects us to meet, as distasteful as some of them might be. Further, our job is to bring the light of God's gospel wherever He might place us without regard to the fact of our rapidly fading liberty. The loss of what we have traditionally deemed as precious and worthy of dying for must be viewed as the natural consequence of a Christ-rejecting, decaying, sin-cursed world that has absolutely no chance of peace and regeneration except through the literal rule of Jesus Christ.

We must accept the fact that the life and citizenship which we have historically cherished will soon fail without equivocation under the weight of human wickedness and will, several years after the taking out of the church, be replaced on this redeemed earth by the real liberty, peace and affluence we look forward to, by faith, through the redemptive work of Jesus Christ. As Livingstone said, "...sever all ties but those that bind me to You". DLM

Chapter 10

Roe vs Wade—35 Years & Counting

~ ~ ~ ~ ~

It was somewhat sobering to watch the counter at the teenshelter.com website. In the few moments I stared at the counter three babies were cut to pieces, scalded or otherwise murdered inside their mother's wombs. At the time this is being written the 35 year total was right at 51.6 million killed since 22 January 1973. This might be a non-issue in the used-to-be hallowed halls of American courts and in the used-to-be rooms of gentle care in medical clinics, but it is not playing well in the Throneroom of Heaven — you can believe that!

Norma McCorvey is the woman that brought it all to a head when her case for an abortion was brought to the U.S. Supreme Court by two young female attorneys, Linda Coffee and Sara Weddington. Known then only as Jane Roe, McCorvey was 21 when the case was filed but never actually had an abortion because her child was born before the case was decided. Actually, she has had three children.

McCorvey, born in Simmesport, LA in 1947, married as a teenager, was divorced and lived in a lesbian relationship from 1970 to 1992 (http://en.wikipedia.org/wiki/Jane_Roe). In 1995 she became a Christian and in 1998 left a Protestant church to become a Catholic. In 2005 she petitioned the Supreme Court to have Roe v. Wade overturned in light of evidence that abortions may harm women, but the court did not grant the hearing.

Occasionally we are asked about children who die from natural causes, or who are murdered while in their mother's wombs. People sometimes wonder about what happens to them. The truth is they go straight into the presence of the Lord, as all innocents do. Jesus said the kingdom of heaven belongs to children (Mark 10:14; see also Deuteronomy 1:39). Parents of aborted children, should they become Christians, will see their children one day when Jesus comes for His church. Things will be much different then; no suffering, no sin, no pain of regret, no sorrow. Those things, and much more, will all be gone and forgotten. For those who are wondering, yes, the grace of God can even cover abortion. No psychiatrist, psychologist, pill or medical procedure can do that. 1 John 1:9—and it costs us nothing! DLM

Chapter 11

School Shootings
The Politically Incorrect Answer

~ ~ ~ ~ ~

Just looking at a broad overview of school shootings it looks like about 100 people have been killed and 141 wounded in school shootings in America since February of 1996, though such violence was present on American campuses even earlier. Some of those who died were the shooters, and if those they killed before getting onto school property are included the number would be slightly higher. Most were teenagers, but one shooter and his victim were both six.

What would cause a girl, age 17, to kill two men, wound eight kids and a police officer by firing into an elementary school in San Diego back in January, 1979? When it was all over she simply shrugged her shoulders and said, "I don't like Mondays." How does a normal person respond to that kind of answer? Does this kind of thing indicate insanity, or does it suggest an ignored, yet sinister influence? The experts search for answers, but it seems their quests are hamstrung from the start by their ingrained biases.

Most experts look for a person, a group, an ideology or an entity of just about any kind to blame no matter how illogical the accusation might be. The idea often seems to be to just find something or someone to pin it on. At times the list of nominees for blame includes conservatively-inclined Christian institutions or people. It is very hard, if not impossible, to find liberal, anti-God groups and ideologies anywhere on a list of those who might have been contributory to such rampages.

On April 20, 1999 Eric Harris and Dylan Klebold killed twelve students, one teacher and wounded 23 others before killing themselves at Columbine High School. They were 18 and 17 respectively, and were part of what they called the "Trench-coat Mafia". They had spent a year planning the assault. Most of us can remember the outcry over that one. One of the first to be assigned blame was the National Rife Association followed by anybody who believes the United States Constitution allows law-abiding citizens to keep and bear arms.

After reading and hearing so much of the tripe being put out by the social engineers I finally responded to an article written by a reporter for Fox News, Barbara Fishkin. She blamed Charlton Heston, the NRA and guns. I had gotten a craw full of her tirade at about that point and wrote her a letter. The following is a portion of it.

...the greater question has to do with why did this happen...Take a kid and bring him up in a home where dad is married to his job and mom-with-a-hyphenated-name is too busy with her career to wipe noses, change diapers, kiss scrapes on the elbow and do all those other things moms could do if they had their priorities in proper order. Teach that kid from K-4 that he is an accident, that his roots go back to some slime-pit somewhere when his ancestors crawled onto dry land, that there is no God and that ultimately there is no accountability.

Tell him there is probably no such place as heaven and there certainly is no such place as hell. Tell him he has no soul, that when he dies he is like a dog — dead and that is it. Combine that with lectures on the brilliance of mankind and his ability to solve all problems with politics, social engineering and money from the federal government. Add it all up and you have a kid set up for disappointment with a big "D". Why? Because if he believes he is an accident, that he did evolve from a lower life form, that there is no loving God who can and will give meaning and hope to all human life that kid will simply have nothing for which to live. And especially so if he sees himself as a victim of some group of "elite" competitors. He will probably hate life and simply see it as fleeting, shallow and of no real consequence. When he gets old enough to see that government, money and the authors of what is politically and socially correct have all failed (as seen in Littleton) he could very well band with others of like mind and together revert to things which give them "the great thrill of life" — killing people. Especially the enemy whom they blame for their every misfortune...

No, lady! It is not Heston, the NRA or guns. Guns were much easier to get when I was a kid...and you know, this kind of thing never happened that I can remember. If you are so determined to blame somebody then put the blame where it belongs — a society which has dismissed God from its classrooms, homes, courts, legislature and the White House.

I would recommend some intellectual honesty, ma'am. This country has changed. The environment in which our kids are raised is rotten. And the horrible truth of the matter is if something is known to work toward ending such putrefaction of American society it is avoided with extreme diligence if it has anything to do with godly morals, the Ten Commandments, prayer, the Bible, etc.

The fact is the humanists have had their day. They have been in charge. They have set the agenda. And they have failed miserably!!! Is it not possible that the only real difference between the Trench-coat Mafia and the social modernists is that the T/M used guns and bombs to destroy 13 people along with themselves, and the humanists are using fallible doctrine and godless philosophy to set up a breeding environment for such killers and would thus destroy an entire nation?

Instead of rationally examining the situation, trying to reverse course in this nation and going back to that which works best, the powers-that-be continue their head-long plunge into this morass of blood, gore and abject amorality, ever intent on forcing upon our people a jaded, miserable, broken-down system which has proven time after time to be a failure. The humanists have failed! Admit it and get on with godly change!

I never received a response from her.

The social engineers decry Christian values that condemn ungodly lifestyles and attitudes, but they wholly support "freedom of expression" as seen on prime-time TV programs that promote homosexuality, music that emphasizes and even glorifies rape, sodomy and the general degradation of women and girls. The gutter-filth heard in so-called rap "music" is excused by saying "...it's a cultural thing". This kind of logic is more than enough to make a normal person vomit, but record producers are churning it out as fast as they can, and parents of teens are letting it into their homes without so much as a blink.

Violent video games have taken the place of books. Few families have meals together and talk. Many kids eat in front of a TV even if their parents are home at the time of the evening meal. Boys like to dress like street thugs with their pants falling off their backsides and girls go to proms showing more skin than a common street walker. (I refer you to the incident several days ago at a New Orleans high school prom).

Movies are filled with nudity, sex acts (heterosexual, homosexual and lesbian) and horror scenes emphasizing bondage and torture with associated shrieks and screams. Painful death is the goal, horror is the means and the big screen is the method of delivery. Bloody massacres and other kinds of evil are shown in detail with the camera occasionally interrupting the carnage only to focus on the dead-pan expression of the killer. All of this, and much more, happens hundreds of thousands of times every day in our country and it has the complete support of the educational, corporate and political powers-that-be.

Then when something like Columbine or VA Tech happens our society's delicate sensitivities are offended and even shocked. Everybody who is somebody quickly finds a microphone and camera and appears on international TV asking, "How could this have happened?" This is where our national hypocrisy comes into full view because no body really wants to be told the truth as to why these things happen. And the reason no body wants to be told the truth is that the answer has to do with our national rejection of God's sovereignty, biblical authority and the Christian worldview.

Just about any old answer will do for the wags who stick their heads in the sand. They want some "expert" to tell them the problem is one of social environment, personality disorders and congressional shortcomings (political talk for not spending enough money on certain issues), and that "...we are working on it right now...". This kind of answer allows them to quickly go back to their movies, music and whatever else it is they like to do while their kids, our country and the world speeds toward wrath, judgment and destruction.

They can be told anything as long as the answer does not include the words God, Bible, repentance or righteousness. Their secular spirits are terribly offended by the use of such words. And, the implication that our nation needs to humbly repent of our godlessness is quite simply too outrageous and reeks of rightwing, religious bigotry that must be destroyed at all costs. Call it anything, they say, but do not make this a spiritual matter!

People do not live in a vacuum — they will live according to what they have been taught and what has been modeled before them. Put another way, a society's world view is directly connected to whatever standard that produces its belief system.

If a person, family, community or nation exchanges the biblical worldview for that which comes from Madison Ave., Hollywood and Darwinism the only possible result is degradation with carnage.

Further, the impact goes beyond the actions of the shooter and can warp the attitude of the victims. By that I mean the victims can actually sympathize with the shooter. I understand a group of VA Tech students has said they do not hold Cho's murdering 32 people against him because he was first and foremost a human being, and that his one bad act should not taint his lifelong reputation. As of print time I could not verify this, but this kind of thinking is not beyond belief.

Most people in the criminal justice professions are familiar with the Stockholm Syndrome whereby hostages identify with their captors. The name comes from the bank robbery/hostage situation in Stockholm that happened in 1973 where the victims defended the criminals after they were freed. It can also be associated with battered wives and other victims of physical and emotional violence.

This kind of warped thinking is emphasized and magnified in our post-modern society where no action can really be labeled as wrong; everything is to be seen as being relative. You see, you become judgmental when you call something wrong, or, God forbid, sin. And everybody knows it is no longer acceptable to pass judgment on other people no matter what they do. This comes from the ages-old lie that there is no such thing as absolutes. Kids learn today that nothing is absolutely right or absolutely wrong because every action of every person is relative to the actions of other people. And that, in turn, is relative to successive and constantly changing standards of conduct. Sounds like unadulterated folly, doesn't it? It is, but we might be surprised at the way this psycho-garbage is being spoon-fed to our kids.

So, why did Cho massacre 32 people? It was not because he

had been picked on. If that were the reason most people would be mass murderers and serial criminals. The simplified answer is he chose to act on his anger in the same way certain movies and music portray reaction to anger — just kill 'em. And his choice to murder 32 innocent people was easily reached because he had been taught in the public school system that we are all animals anyway, that we all have a single slime-ball as an ancestor, and we are not much different from chimpanzees. He probably had been taught there is no life-after-death and that this heaven/hell thing is just the musings and fantasies of weaklings who need religion, the opiate of ignorant and common people. Reminds me of what a man named Stalin did and the reasons he did it.

Did he have a mental illness? Perhaps, but such an illness does not excuse murder. That is, he still made a choice. Pedophiles are said to be ill, yet they do not do their wicked deeds in the presence of adults which indicates they understand what they are doing and simply make choices as to when is the best time to attack innocent children. In most cases the word "evil" is more accurate than "ill".

Dr. Helen Smith, a forensic psychologist in Knoxville, TN, says the blame should not be on violent TV, songs from rock groups, etc. She says violent acts result "...from the accumulation of many distorted thoughts and stressors that finally send a child over the edge. In short it is the way he or she processes what they see, hear and experience..." They see violence as, "the best mode of action" (crimelibrary.com/serial_killers/weird/kids1/say_say5html). No kidding?

Yet, that still does not address the root of the problem. What has happened in the last 50 years to change the way a teenager thinks? What is the standard by which kids process what they see, etc.? Where did they learn that violence is sometimes the best way to handle things? Do you think maybe rap music, horror movies and gutter-level moral standards have anything to do with it? Do you think a nation's mostly godless entertainment industry plays a role?

Massacres have always been a part of human history, but what is happening in our country seems to be quite different. These things are not happening because of religious hatred (as was the case in Beslan in 2004 when Moslems slaughtered 186 children in that school siege) or even political disagreements. Columbine and VA Tech betray something more ominous because they result from a society that has declared its independence from God. Nothing — absolutely nothing — robs the human heart of civility and compassion and smashes the moral compass of the human conscience like alienation from God.

That we are living in the shadow of Revelation 6 is without question in my opinion. Such massacres are simply the beginning of tribulation birth pangs which, I believe, will become more frequent and more intense. For non-Christians this is a horrible scenario. For Christians it promotes great anticipation. DLM

Chapter 12

José dé Jesús

~ ~ ~ ~ ~

In 1973 two angels went to Jose de Jesus in a vision and imparted to him the same spirit that was in Jesus of Nazareth. Thus, he says, he became the messiah.

Jose de Jesus is gathering quite a following these days. People are falling all over themselves in some thirty countries just to get near him. Some of them fall to the floor in tears when he preaches. So, what does he preach that can impact people so strongly? There is no more sin, no devil and no need to pray because you can do no wrong in God's eyes. Just what the crowd wants to hear. If it were not so serious this would be better than a circus act.

When asked who he is, Jose says, "Jesus Christ, man, the second manifestation, the Second Coming of Christ." He also calls himself Anti-Christ — not some evil man, but the final incarnation of Jesus on earth. Some of his followers even have "666" tattooed on their bodies so that "...everyone knows my life belongs to the man."

Because most people see this charlatan and his teachings as some kind of comic act, something very important is being over looked. If de Jesus can get people from all over the world to believe he is the Christ and to take a mark that is biblically associated with the coming anti-Christ (whom he is not!), how difficult will it be for the real anti-Christ to convince the world to do so when they will have every reason based on human logic to do so? It probably will not be hard at all. If a shallow fake like de Jesus can do this much, what do you think the real anti-Christ (empowered personally by Satan) will be able to do?

Jesus said in the end times many will come claiming to be the messiah (Matthew 24:4, 5). We are there now though most Christians ignore all the evidence. That is sad, indeed. Because they refuse to take Bible prophecy literally many Christians are being put to sleep by the modern emphasis upon allegory, replacement theology, "seeker" churches, feel-good religion, etc. They slumber as the greatest moment in the last 2000 years rapidly approaches — the rapture of the church. Somehow the word "sad" does not adequately describe it.

Chapter 13

Mardi Gras
Connected to End Time Events

~ ~ ~ ~ ~

If a person is familiar with the Mardi Gras season and its associated activities it is not unreasonable to ask if this infamous
celebration might have any connection or association with the
culture of the end times. Perhaps it does.

Mardi Gras stems from Roman and Greek paganism, is deeply
rooted in what is loosely called "Christian" tradition, teaches
the concept of play-and-pay, encourages the rankest of moral
degradation, extends toleration to virtually every form of devi-
ant behavior, saps a lot of time and energy in preparation and
brings in a lot of money to private and public coffers. Thus, it
seems it would fit quite nicely in those religious and financial
activities associated with the end-times and wretchedly vile religious prostitute of Revelation 17 and 18.

Mardi Gras, or Carnival as it is called in some places, is celebrated in many major cities of the world such as Venice, Rio De
Janeiro and Munich where it is known as Fasching. The common denominator, though, is it is a time of revelry that provides
both license and opportunity for just about any kind of conduct
imaginable just before the Lenten season begins at midnight on
Ash Wednesday.

During Mardi Gras revelers take liberties to really get down and dirty just before Lent because when Lent begins it suddenly becomes sin. You know, sort of the "last hoorah" before getting religious. According to Wikipedia the purpose of Lent is to prepare the believer - through prayer, penitence, almsgiving and self-denial - for the commemoration of the death and resurrection of Jesus (http://en.wikipedia.org/wiki/Lent). So, Mardi Gras gives official license to a person to reduce their moral standard of living to that of a pot-licker hound, and then on Ash Wednesday to become remorseful, go to church, ask forgiveness and do an act of contrition so that everything suddenly becomes OK between them and God.

Is it really that bad, or is the above just an embellishment of the facts? If a person has ever been to Mardi Gras in New Orleans that question would not have to be asked. Still, consider what others have said.

John Edward Koerner III, Krewe of Rex, in an interview with WDSU TV 6, said that at Mardi Gras people "...waive about half the Ten Commandments..." and that "People choose to waive what commandments they wish." That is an interesting comment since the celebration is deeply rooted with what most people call Christianity. But, is it really Christianity?

Not at all. Nobody, religious leader or not, can point to any scripture that even hints that God's prohibitions against drunkenness, fornication, adultery, homosexuality, etc., can be waived to any degree by anyone for any reason. If that is true, what makes people believe they can do those things with impunity? The answer is in two parts. First, many religious leaders say it is OK. And second, great numbers of people want license to do what they are going to do anyway. Having it associated with religion, you see, salves their consciences.

Does this not remind us of the direction the false "Christian" religious world is going presently, whose vileness and destruction are seen in Revelation 17 and 18? People are being told that tolerance is now god, that to condemn any one's conduct is too judgmental and that as long as everything is consensual and nobody gets hurt there is really no harm done. What we have here is the old, "Well, God understands." kind of thinking.

One tourist described the 2008 New Orleans Mardi Gras this way (verbatim except for obvious editing): *Sixty year old women walk about topless, with elaborate designs painted on their chests, and teenage boys pause to gawk and take pictures...Balconies sponsored by Trojan, Bacardi and Frat Boyz are filled with virile youth. Crowds gather on the street below them, and they engage in a base conversation, where beads, breasts and vulgar gestures take the place of words and phrases...A very hairy man who is clearly wearing nothing but over-sized extra-large overalls...wanders about, allowing glimpses of his full profile...women in short tight skirts dance with him...girls act coy but secretly pleased to get cat calls, "Show me your ____! Show me your ____!" The street smells literally like human waste...people are finding themselves and enjoying life as only the very lonely and the very drunk can. For some reason the smiles seem sad, the cat calls seem disinterested...I always thought Bourbon St. and the French Quarter to be a happy place. But call it the heeby jeebies, call it psychic intuition, call it whatever you will: this place drains my spirit, it sucks away my happiness and I will be glad to leave this city...tomorrow.* This, folks, is the truth about Mardi Gras in a nutshell.

It is impossible to fully address this subject with such limited space, yet it is necessary to take some of that space to make a note at this point. Lest anyone misunderstand, there are any number of Mardi Gras parades that are family-friendly with people who do not subscribe to the raunchiness most often publicized by the media. Yet, when one steps back and objectively examines the whole idea of pre-Lenten revelry that one quickly sees that at the core of even those more pleasant events lies the same kernel that gives life to the depraved and lurid side of the show.

Though I have seen Fasching, and it is very similar to Mardi Gras, yet naturally I am most familiar with the Louisiana version. The French Catholic heritage of Mardi Gras came to Louisiana by way of the Le Moyne brothers, Pierre Le Moyne d'Iberville and Jean-Baptiste Le Moyne de Bienville in the late 1600s. About 60 miles downriver from New Orleans, on March 3, 1699 Iberville stopped at a place where a small bayou drained into the Mississippi from the west bank, and named the spot Point du Mardi Gras (Mardi Gras point) in honor of the holiday. The tradition took root and has prospered like a weed ever since.

During the tribulation God will send two witnesses to be placed at the epi-center of the action on earth at that time (Revelation 11:3ff). These men will call attention to man's sin and God's wrath, and no doubt to the rottenness of the prevailing and false church. Mardi Gras was not without something similar. FoxNews.com featured a story on Wednesday, February 6th that mentioned a Christian group preaching on Bourbon Street. Douglas Barry held up a large sign (you might have seen it on some TV reports) warning the raucous crowd their actions was the doorway to hell. Barry said, "Not everyone welcomes our message, but people never needed to hear it more than today." Barry's group was mostly ignored, but one reveler said, "He told me I was headed to hell, but all I'm doing is wandering around taking in the sights. He said that makes me a dirty old man, which is probably true, but I'm a happy one today."

We have not been told all the details of the harlot religion of Revelation 17, but the connection between it and what we see presently is undeniable. The forerunner of the harlot church is much more than simply a single, specific church. It includes all that we see as vile corruptions of Christianity. It is an attitude and practice that lays claim to Christianity with certain liturgical buzz words and panoply, but which at its core reeks of paganism. It has the pomp and circumstance of world-class religion with wealth, power, bright colors, intrigue and mystery, but at its essence it is like a ruptured wormy cyst filled with putrefaction, filth and a foul stench that causes the godly to gag.

The false church will not only be tolerant but also tolerated. She will be endured by anti-Christ for obvious reasons, but will, in reality, be hated with a passion. When anti-Christ has used her to the fullest he will then destroy her with fervor and rage (Revelation 17:16). Tyrants have no personal interest in religion of any kind, but they are not so stupid as to not recognize the usefulness of religion in the pacification of the masses. If stupidity is to be found in any of the world-wide entities of the tribulation period, it will be found in this harlot church which believes she will maintain control over the religious and economic aspects of anti-Christ's kingdom. What a revolting development it will be for this false religious church empire to be suddenly destroyed. The commercial world will be horrified (Revelation 18:8ff). That which was so used to great power and wealth will suddenly become hated and quickly reduced to ashes.

The roots of the economic relationship this coming world harlot church will have with anti-Christ's government is present today in several ways. Specifically, that a church can and will issue both license and absolution for unrestrained lust is an important part of overall economic considerations today and in the future. Its all about money and power.

Think about it. Why do the city fathers not denounce the degradation of carnival? Why does New Orleans Mayor Ray Nagin openly welcome Southern Decadence, the yearly Labor Day homosexual party in New Orleans?

One does not have to be very smart to figure out that one. Note the following quote from the Southern Decadence website: *Southern Decadence started thirty-seven years ago as a simple going-away party. As a top gay Labor Day Weekend destination, it has evolved into one of our world's major annual events. One of the largest annual celebrations in New Orleans, it has become known as the Gay Mardi Gras."People begin to arrive on the Wednesday before Labor Day, and generally don't even think about stopping or going home until the following Tuesday.* *With over 100,000 gay, lesbian, bisexual and transgender participants, the economic impact on the city was estimated to be in excess of $95 million.* *The city has recognized its importance with an Official Proclamation to welcome the event.* (Emphasis mine.)

Prior to Hurricane Katrina the economic impact from Mardi Gras was $250 million. It is near that level presently if not more. Is there any wonder the city fathers do nothing to discourage the activities of Mardi Gras? Their thinking is that a few days of gutter-level filth is not too much to tolerate for a return of $250 million.

Perhaps even more to the point is the fact that anyone who might take issue with the moral climate of Mardi Gras will quickly find themselves in a confrontation with the religious powers-that-be. To indict Mardi Gras is to indict the area's French/Catholic heritage, and that would be the economic and social death-knell for any business or politician. See: "Catholic Roots of Mardi Gras" at http://americancatholic.org/Features/MardiGras/default.asp

So, how can otherwise "religious" people buy into this kind of reprobate living? Simple. Over thirty-five years ago a woman took it upon herself to talk to a fellow student about her sleazy lifestyle. She asked this Bible-carrying, church-going, loud-praying friend how she could claim to be a Christian while doing a lot of heavy partying and sleeping with a different man every weekend. Her friend smiled broadly and said, "Oh, Jane, you just don't understand. That's why Jesus died for us!"

The modern religious world shows us something we need to get straight. The idea that the false church of the tribulation period will be some sort of aberration that will repel people with its leadership, worship protocols, indulgencies, etc., is not accurate. That false church will be as much a part of the God-hating, post-rapture world as Mom, the flag and apple pie were to Americans of the 1950s. In fact, the world will be so dazzled by anti-Christ that people will not be able to believe everybody is not worshipping him (Revelation 13:3, 4). We see this same way of thinking every time a "religious" persons says, "I can't believe you don't want to go to Bourbon Street for Mardi Gras!"

Will things get better? No. A hurricane is strengthened when it moves into the right conditions like seasoned, warm tropical waters. The foundation for the harlot church is being strengthened each day as the moment of the rapture gets nearer. Worldwide religious, political and economic conditions are presently seasoned and ripe for the introduction of anti-Christ and his hideous false religion. I venture to say when the harlot church of the tribulation comes onto the scene it won't be a dramatic change from what we see today, but rather it will be just one more step, one more gradation from the present condition.

I know of no reputable Bible prophecy teacher who sees the anti-Christ behind every bush, or who knows his and the false prophet's identities. Beware of such charlatans, for God has not chosen to give us such details. But, there are two things we must keep in mind as Christians living in these last days. First, to ignore the obvious is to not take seriously those things God has chosen to reveal to us. And second, to be so timid as to refrain from bringing those matters to light is to be derelict in our duty.

So, in the analysis are religious celebrations like Mardi Gras and their associated corrupt practices connected in some way to post-rapture events? In my opinion, yes. DLM

Chapter 14

The Night Belshazzar Died – déjà vu?

~ ~ ~ ~ ~

It is nothing less than amazing to see how God works in the affairs of people and nations. Judah went into captivity to Babylon because of her unbelief and rebellion, thus God used the evil Babylonians to punish them (Jeremiah 20). At the same time, however, He said the Babylonians would also be punished for the way they would treat His people during their captivity (Jeremiah 25). From this we learn that though God does not deny the free-will of humans, He uses that same free-will to accomplish that which He has ordained to be. A good case in point is the story of Belshazzar found in Daniel chapter five. It all happened on the night of October 29th, 539 BC.

Belshazzar was a reckless, intemperate and confirmed pleasure-seeker who was probably spoiled rotten as a child. His father, Nabonidus, was somewhat of a cultured man who had basically gone into retirement and left his arrogant son in charge of the kingdom. On that particular night Belshazzar gave a big party for his nobles and everybody who was somebody in Babylon. It became a drunken orgy with all his wives and concubines present. If that were not bad enough he decided, for specific reasons unknown, to blaspheme the God of Israel. He commanded the gold vessels taken from Solomon's temple in Jerusalem be brought in and that everybody should drink from them. The king, with joyous spirit, went on to praise the gods of gold and silver. This blasphemous party was the last straw and God finally took action and intervened.

During the party and without warning a hand appeared and wrote something on the wall next to where Belshazzar was sitting. The hand then disappeared just as suddenly as it appeared. Such an event cannot make a drunken man sober, but it can indeed make a drunken man fearful. In fact, Belshazzar was so scared that his knees knocked together. He offered a great reward to anyone who could interpret the writing, but none of his "wise men" had a clue as to what was going on. The aged Daniel was finally brought in and was offered the position of being third in command to Nabonidus if he could interpret the meaning.

The first thing the prophet Daniel did was to rebuke the king for his pride and blasphemy and then he told him he did not want the rewards. He told Belshazzar the inscription meant he had been weighed in the balance by God and had been found wanting. As a result the king's realm would be given to the Medes and Persians, his enemies.

Then what happened next is the interesting part. Belshazzar accepted the interpretation and insisted that Daniel be given the rewards: the purple robe, the necklace of gold and the place of being third in the kingdom. The text indicates Belshazzar had no anger toward Daniel and, more importantly, no ominous sense of foreboding. Yet, that very night some soldiers of the Medo-Persian army diverted the Euphrates River which flowed beneath the city walls, walked in and took the city. Belshazzar, while drinking from God's golden cups and reveling in his pagan kingship, was killed that very night.

What was the problem with Belshazzar? Actually, he had three major problems. He failed to learn the lesson about Nebuchadnezzar regarding how God deals with arrogance and pride (Daniel 4). He did not really believe God would intervene in the affairs of men, and he did not believe in the imminence of God's judgment, if any would even come at all. He was a fool.

The life and death of Belshazzar presents us with an excellent pre-type of the Gentile-ruled world of the last days. As much as any man in history he exemplifies the attitude of the anti-God system that will exist in those days just prior to the removal of the church from the world by way of the rapture. By taking a look at Belshazzar and superimposing his attitude upon our modern secular society, it becomes easy to see just how reflective things are today of that ancient evil king and the wickedness of his day.

In the days of Belshazzar God was of no genuine concern. Though some of the pagan Babylonians acknowledged the existence of Jehovah, the God of the Jews, they did not really pay much attention to Him. To most of them He was just another god to be given a measure of recognition, but to whom would be given no serious credibility much less worship and heed.

In the culture of the 21st century it seems this attitude is even more pronounced. That is, though the pagan king Nebuchadnezzar acknowledged the power of God (Daniel 4:34ff) 2500 years ago, modernists often do not even believe in God. It has been reported there are over 205 million atheists in the world and about 30 million in America.[1] The die-hards among these people will not be swayed by the obviously God-made complexity of nature, the unassailable credibility of the Bible nor the loving and selfless example of Christian friends. Their hearts have been so deadened by the poison of humanism that even the disappearance of millions of people at the rapture will likewise have no genuine and lasting impact on their belief system. Secularists go beyond simply not learning lessons from the past about God — they refuse to believe He even exists.

You see, to believe in God as the only God is to acknowledge He just might have something to say about the way people should live. And for the secularist this is anathema. No secularist in his right mind in this post-modern world would dare admit to consulting God about anything much less heeding anything He might say. This is the major problem with evolution. That is, a growing number of researchers associated with the life sciences admits the theory of evolution has too many holes in it to be believable. Yet, at the same time they reject the concept of "intelligent design" because it would force them to admit the reality of God, and if that is admitted then logic would require them to at least consider what He has to say. And that is simply unacceptable.

Since Daniel's interpretation was not to Belshazzar's benefit, why did Belshazzar not kill him immediately? One reason is that Belshazzar did have a type of religious belief system, though it was definitely pagan to the core, and as a result he might have granted at least a measure of interest to what Daniel had said. He had certainly been taught the history of Babylon under Nebuchadnezzar, and Daniel's name was not entirely foreign to him. But, Belshazzar chose to severely limit whatever interest that might have been in his heart.

Many people think along this same line today. They have some sort of belief system that lays the groundwork for at least a cursory nod to the Bible, though they would classify it as a work of literature instead of the Word of God. These people feel the stories of the great miracles of God are at best myths with nice morals but are definitely not truths with consequences. The immutable laws of God are smiled at condescendingly and His warnings about imminent judgment are classified as the tirades of an angry god conjured up by the imagination of people too uncouth, uneducated and unsophisticated to escape the clutches of superstition. God is simply not taken seriously, if He is even believed in at all.

Belshazzar did not believe Daniel's God would actually take a hand in his personal matters and those of his kingdom. Thus, he might have been an ancient deist. That is, he might have admitted the existence of God, but he refused to really believe He is in any way involved in the affairs of this world. Lots of people are like that today. And, it is incumbent upon Christians to issue the warning to those people: do not fail to notice that God has previously intervened several times in the natural course of human events and He has specific plans to intervene several times more in the future.

This is a type of template for God; that is, He has intervened in the past, and He will do so again. This is critical to an accurate understanding of Bible prophecy.

God is indeed interested in what happens to this world. He made it, and He has plans for it. Do not think for one second He has removed His hand from the affairs of the planet. This is somewhat difficult for many people to accept. And a major reason for their rejection of this truth is they know precious little, at best, about the matter. These folks know more about the stock market, the weeknight sit-com schedule, the NFL draft and Washington politics than they do about what God has said regarding the future. They have little or no faith because they avoid that which brings faith (Romans 10:17). Bible prophecy to them is foreign to their thinking, uncomfortable in any discussion, distressing in its analysis and dreadful in its fulfillment.

If Belshazzar really believed anything Daniel said would happen at all, he did not believe it would happen right away. After all, he was secure behind those massive city walls with an abundance of food and water, and his army was on guard ready to repel any invader. He placed his trust in his own wisdom, his own gods and his own security measures. But mostly Belshazzar trusted his own intuition which said nothing will happen any time soon; eat, drink and have a good time for tomorrow will be like today, only better.

Can you imagine his surprise when the Medes and Persians came bursting into his throne room that same night? In gut-wrenching fear he might have screamed, "No!" in disbelief as the soldiers quickly moved upon him to drive swords or spears into his belly. When his great party began earlier that same evening his impending and violent death was the farthest thing from his pagan mind. Oh, how quickly can horrifying events happen, and how permanent the results!

Like the appearance of the Medes and Persians in Belshazzar's throne room, the rapture of the church will also be an absolute and total surprise to untold multitudes. Some of those surprised will know what has happened, but it will be altogether too late. Most, however, will not understand and will therefore be open to the lies that will be spoon fed to them by all the false and apostate religious leaders who will also be left behind.

So, when this happens will there be any who will not be surprised? That is an easy question. Those who get up each morning and who go to bed each evening thinking, "This might be the day." will not be caught by surprise. It will be the consummate answer to their fervent prayer, *Maranatha*! (1 Corinthians 16:22).

Even some professing Christians (a loose term in this context) refuse to believe in what we call the rapture. As was the case with Noah's neighbors, with Korah and others like them, a very big and terrible surprise is waiting for them right around the corner! No prophecy must be fulfilled first, no event in Israel must happen first and the anti-Christ will not appear first. Plainly said: it could happen at any moment.

The "yes, but not now" attitude is quite common in these last days. Many of these same people were taught the truth in their early years about sin, judgment, the cross, the rapture, etc., but as they grew older they put aside such "childish" things. Essentially their hearts became calloused and the conviction of the Holy Spirit no longer had any effect. Somewhere, deeply embedded in the recesses of their memory, lies the truth about the rapture, the tribulation, judgment, etc., but they seldom think about such things and their already hardened hearts are salved by Satan's lie that says, "Yes, it's okay to believe in all that, but just don't take it seriously. And, besides, all that prophecy stuff is probably a thousand years away. And besides, you are still young..."

The 2500 year old story of Belshazzar is being repeated in these last days. Only this time the character is not a specific man, but an entire world of people. And the consequences will not be limited to the taking of a city and the death of its king, but the entire planet with billions of people will be thrown into a seven year time of suffering and death that is absolutely unprecedented. Though certainly not void of a heart-felt attitude of love for lost people, the Daniels of today understand that the time for politically correct, milquetoast diplomacy is over. Now is the time to say what must be said. Déjà vu? Yes! DLM

End Note:
1) "Number of Atheists". www.religioustolerance.org/atheist1.htm. Cited 21 April 05

Chapter 15

God's *Signature*

~ ~ ~ ~ ~

Historically people have always used some means of authenticating their authorship of a document or masterpiece. Artisans usually signed their masterpieces and kings usually sealed their decrees by pressing their stamps into soft wax or clay. In today's world we sign documents and letters, and in the case of papers that require legal status we sign them in the presence of a notary, whose signature and seal vouch for their authenticity.

This is especially helpful in those cases where a signatory has handwriting that is impossible to understand. And that is the interesting thing about signatures on legal documents — they are not there to be understood, but rather to be recognized. God, too, has a signature that He affixes to His work, and it is vastly different from anything anyone else might use. God's signature is always the miraculous.

Go back to the beginning and remember that God spoke the universe into existence. He created the world *ex nihilo*, out of nothing. No human can understand this because we have been taught that energy and matter cannot be created nor destroyed — it simply changes form (first law of thermodynamics). Yet, God made everything from nothing. A miracle.

Many who believe in evolution are atheists and, therefore, say

God had nothing to do with life. They believe there can be no miraculous signature of a God that does not exist. Today, an increasing number of scientists are questioning evolution because they clearly see it falls flat when held to the light of honest evaluation. Most of them, however, are not ready to fully discard the theory because they would be forced to accept the fact that some great designer made this world, and that great designer is none other than God. This they simply cannot accept, and they are left in their self-made quandary. They deny the miraculous.

So, the very first time we see God's signature is in creation. Whether one examines the smallest one-celled living creature, or the solar system and universe, there is only one conclusion that can be drawn. And that conclusion is this did not just happen; there had to be a powerful designer involved. Paul, in Romans 1:18-23, quite simply cut the argument to its core: no one can be excused for not believing in God because the creation itself declares His existence. If a person is mentally able to make simple observations and draw simple conclusions that person cannot help but know God exists. The miracle of creation proves it.

Yet, creation is not the only miracle God has used for His signature down through the millennia. The ancient Hebrews saw another one. God, through Moses, led two million people out of slavery in Egypt into the Promised Land. They were divinely protected during the Passover, they crossed the Red Sea on dry land, they were fed with manna from heaven, their clothes did not wear out in the desert, they were led by fire and a cloud, etc.

Stephen, in his defense before the Sanhedrin, referred to this great miracle (Acts 7:36ff). It was an irrefutable event categorically accepted by the Jewish people. Even their enemies in Canaan knew the facts of the story and they became fearful and trembled at their approach (Joshua 2:8-11). The exodus is still referred to today by religious Jews as authentication of God's existence and His relationship with the people.

But, there is yet another miracle that will be referred to in the not-so-distant future as the by-word for God's power and presence among His people. Jeremiah 16:14, 15 says, *Therefore behold, days are coming,"declares the Lord, When it will no longer be said, 'As the Lord lives, who brought up the sons of Israel out of the land of Egypt,' but,' As the Lord lives, who brought up the sons of Israel from the land of the north and from all the countries where He had banished them.' For I will restore them to their own land which I gave to their fathers.*

There is absolutely no doubt that we are presently witnessing the greatest miracle ever concerning God's dealings with the people of Israel. Never before in the history of the world has a nation that has been in the dust bin of history for nearly 1900 years been raised up and restored to its ancient homeland. But Israel has. Another miracle.

In AD 70 the people of Judea were dispersed around the world by the Romans who had captured Jerusalem under the leadership of Pompey in 64 BC. The city of Jerusalem was destroyed and their Temple was burned. The 134 day siege came to an end when the entire city was put to fire. The Jews who were left in their land after AD 70 built a few modest structures in Jerusalem, but soon even those were destroyed. In AD 132 a man named Bar-Cochba claimed to be the Messiah and led a revolt against the Romans. This time they destroyed everything, even those small structures that had be rebuilt since AD 70. At that time the remaining stones from the Temple complex were pulled down. Just as Jesus had predicted, not one stone was left upon another.

By AD 135 Judea was completely denationalized. In the minds of all the Gentiles this was it. The Jewish nation was now only a part of history, and the Jewish people would soon be assimilated into host cultures around the world. The thought that God would work a miracle and bring them back to their ancient homeland, something clearly taught in the Old Testament, was hands-down rejected.

And the land became desolate. As late as 1867 the land was a virtual disaster. Mark Twain visited the land in that year and wrote that it was a "...desolate country, whose soil is rich enough, but is given over wholly to weeds...A desolation is here that not even imagination can grace with the pomp of life and action." He further said that the country "...sits in sackcloth and ashes. Over it broods a spell of a curse that has withered its fields and fettered its energies." He said the land was desolate and, though important to poetry and tradition, it was simply useless. [1]

In the late 1800s God began to move in the hearts of certain leaders in Europe about having a homeland for the wandering Jew. Zionism was born in those days, and under the leadership of such men as Theodor Herzl it slowly began to spread. A God-ordained longing was conceived in the hearts of many Jewish people to have a homeland of their own; specifically, to have their own land again. Persecution in Europe against the Jews woke some of them up to their need, but most were still determined to stay among the Gentiles.

The events of World War 1 were used by God to make a place ready for His people in their own homeland. The events of World War 2 were used by God to prepare His people for a land of their own. Only after the devastation of Nazism were the Jews finally ready to admit there was only one people they could trust with their lives — fellow Jews, and there was only place they could go where they could seek peace, nationhood and the right to defend themselves — Israel. God placed a su-pernatural longing in their hearts for their ancient homeland.

Contrary to the international lie, the area was not claimed as sovereign territory by the surrounding Arab nations. Said an-other way, it was not within the borders of Egypt, Jordan, Syria, etc. The Arabs living there did not call themselves Palestinians because there was no such thing as a state of Palestine. They mostly referred to themselves as Syrians living outside the bor-ders of Syria. The League of Nations and the United Nations

both understood the situation and assigned the place as a homeland for the Jews. And it was then that the real trouble began.

It all came to a head on May 14, 1948. After the British Com-
missioner left the area that day (not before leaving most of the
British military hardware in the hands of the Arabs), at 4:00PM
the modern State of Israel was declared. Part of the declaration
reads: "...we...are here assembled on the day of the termination
of the British Mandate over Eretz-Israel and, by virtue of our
national and historic right and on the strength of the Resolution
of the United Nations General Assembly hereby declare the establishment of a Jewish state in Eretz-Israel, to be known as the
State of Israel."[2] A miracle in no uncertain terms! And note the
final sentence of the declaration: "The State of Israel will be
open for Jewish immigration and for the ingathering of the ex-
iles." This is *exactly* what God said would happen, almost
down to the very words used in the declaration!

And this is the great miracle: that God resurrected a nation that
was seen as lifeless by the world, and not only did He resurrect
that nation, but He brought them to their ancient homeland, as
He said He would. Remember the words of God to Ezekiel in
chapter 37. *Thus says the Lord God to these bones, 'Behold, I
will cause breath to enter you that you may come to life. And I
will put sinews on you, make flesh grow back on you, cover you
with skin, and put breath in you that you may come alive; and
you will know that I am the Lord'"*(Ezekiel 37:5,6). And lest
someone wonder if God was talking about the nation of Israel,
*Then He said to me, Son of man, these bones are the whole
house of Israel; behold, they say, 'Our bones are dried up, and
our hope has perished. We are completely cut off.' Therefore
prophesy, and say to them, 'Thus says the Lord God,"Behold, I
will open your graves and cause you to come up out of your
graves, My people; and I will bring you into the land of Israel*
(37:11,12 emphasis mine).

God's signature is no longer the exodus; it is now the return!
And their return is continuing today. The government of Israel

is taking in and making room for tens of thousands of Jews from all over the world every year. Many of those Jews say they immigrated to Israel because of what they call a sense of longing in their hearts for their ancient homeland. It is as if they cannot fully explain it; they just know they wanted to go "home". Of course we know why. God Himself has placed that longing in their hearts. It is all part of His great plan. One day in the not-too-distant future they will ...*look upon Me whom they Pierced; and they will mourn for Him, as one mourns for an only son, and they will weep bitterly over Him, like the bitter weeping over a first-born* (Zechariah 12:10). God said, *They will call on My name, and I will answer them; I will say, 'They are My people', and they will say, 'The Lord is my God'"* (Zechariah 13:9).

The fact that the Jewish nation has been reestablished does not fit into the theological thinking of most people in the world. But that does not matter. What matters is that He is doing this great miracle. Many people, and among them the majority of Christians, vehemently deny what is happening, but it cannot be logically denied; it can only be believed. The promise is sealed and signed by God's own hand. It is not up for debate and it is not something that can be spiritualized in some contorted way and applied to the church. It is the fulfillment of God's promises to a people very special to Him and very instrumental in His plan for the ages. The return is His signature. And though many cannot understand it, there should be no question that everyone should be able to recognize it. DLM

End Notes:
1) Mark Twain, *The Innocents Abroad* (New York, 1966), pp 351, 375, 401, 441
2) John Phillips, *Exploring the World of the Jew* (Neptune, NJ: Loizeaux Brothers, revised 1993), pp 145-6, "The Declaration of the Establishment of the State of Israel"

Chapter 16

Israel—60 Years Toward Forever

~ ~ ~ ~ ~

May 14, 1948 is the day Israel became a nation again. The Arabs call it "naqba", Arabic for catastrophe, and for the most part the entire world agrees. Though not everyone wants to see Israel nuked by the Arabs, yet general thinking is that things would be much better on this planet if Israel had quite simply been destroyed at her birth.

Headlines on many news websites today are announcing the continued plight of "displaced Arabs" who are still confined to refugee camps as a result of the 1948 War of Independence. On each anniversary world media focus on lost houses, lands and businesses in their undying efforts to portray the whole struggle for Israeli independence and acceptance as a horrible exercise in Jewish domination of the loving and peaceful Arab people and the land of their heritage.

Is that, in fact, the truth? Is it the real picture? Or, is it Arab propaganda orchestrated to play on the emotions of a world that hates the Jews to begin with? Most people, and sadly many Christians, are not only neck-deep in ignorance regarding the facts surrounding the reestablishment of Israel, but when they are brought face-to-face with the truth they steadfastly refuse to accept it. It is nothing less than amazing to see how deeply rooted anti-Semitism is in the hearts of so many Christians who, at the same time, loudly claim allegiance to the world's greatest Jew, Jesus.

Most preachers very seldom, if ever, expound Bible prophecy in general, much less specific texts relative to the re-birth of Israel. For some of them just being reminded of the Israeli state is hateful in their thinking. Do you suppose my words might be a little too strong? Not at all! On several occasions I have seen self-described conservative, evangelical preachers grimace at the mention of Israel and nearly spit out the accusation, "God is finished with the Jews, and they are just criminals in that land they stole from those poor Arabs!" Though it is almost beyond belief, yet many self-professing Christians are blindly buying into that same world-class lie.

Further, holocaust-denying has become the in-vogue thing among the anti-Semitic elite, and it is becoming a mainstream idea even in some churches. One such semi-famous radio "Bible teacher" said to me in a telephone conversation, "The Nazis didn't do it...it is all just a Zionist lie...the Allies are responsible for the deaths of the Jews in the camps because the U.S. Army Air Corp was always strafing the railroads and prevented the SS from getting food and medicine to the Jews in the camps!" With such a warped belief system becoming so common it is no wonder America's pulpits are silent about the Jews, Israel and the rebirth of their nation. It is amazing how some Christians willingly buy into this bold-faced lie, and at the same time soundly reject the clear truth of prophecy!

The 60th anniversary of the most important prophetic fulfillment of the 20th century will go unnoticed in the overwhelming majority of pulpits, Bible classes, lesson commentaries, etc. It does not even rate a quick blip on the radar screen of modern Christendom. Why might this be the case? Perhaps there are too many other issues demanding our attention presently; things more feel-good and social in nature than biblical.

Additionally, many preachers and church leaders are more interested in those issues of personal opinion that they have been made into icons of division and sectarianism that must be addressed on a regular basis in order to keep people on what they deem is the right track. It is both sad and frustrating that many of the same people who will fight to the death over the issue of musical instruments in the assembly, the number of cups in the Communion service or having a kitchen facility in a church building will willingly roll over and buy into anti-Semitism without giving it a second thought.

Back in 1948 America played a very significant role in the reestablishment of the Israeli state, and the account of how this all worked together is a rather amazing story. Space will not allow sufficient attention to the details, so we will get just an overview in this newsletter.

I believe the events surrounding the presidency of Harry S. Truman were orchestrated by the hand of God. The details would require a book, but the gist is God put Truman in the White House "for such a time as this" (Esther 4:14). In 1948, when the British pulled out of so-called Palestine, Truman was under intense pressure to not recognize Israel. The entire world knew the Jews were going to declare their independence and that war would no doubt break out.

The critical moment regarding Israel's survival from the international political perspective would be when Truman would say either "yea" or "nay"; to recognize the newly born State of Israel or to not recognize her. If he would not, the Arabs would have a much easier job of destroying her, for non-recognition would block Israel's legitimacy in the eyes of the world and the result would be isolation and no support in the war effort. But, if Truman said "yes", then the weight and credibility of the U.S. would be behind the new nation.

Many years before Truman became president God allowed his path to cross that of a Jew named Eddie Jacobson while they were in the Army posted at Camp Doniphan near Lawton, Oklahoma. Later they went into business together, a haberdashery. A close friendship between the two was formed in those days; a friendship that would prove vital to Israel's recognition later.

In 1948 Jacobson, who never used his friendship with Truman for self promotion and who also knew the pressure Truman was under to not recognize Israel, asked his old friend to hear what another Jew had to say about Israel's quest for independence. This man was a very famous British chemist named Dr. Chaim Wiseman. The facts that Wiseman presented along with the urging of his special counsel, Clark M. Clifford, all helped Truman come to his decision to grant U.S. recognition.

But, there is no question that the hand of God was there, overruling the pro-Arab arguments of Secretary of State George Marshall and working in the quiet recesses of the President's heart that only he could hear and appreciate. The result was Israel made their declaration at 4:00PM and the U.S. issued the recognition at 4:05PM.

That God sees the beginning from the end is a no-brainer. That He also sets in motion seemingly benign events in the lives of His people for later use and impact is also a no-brainer. Nobody knows very much about the seemingly insignificant conversations between Field Artillery Lt. Harry Truman and his company clerk, Pvt. Edward Jacobson, but history clearly reveals they might not have been so insignificant. That they eventually went into business together and maintained a lifelong friendship is no insignificant result of mundane conversations. It would appear that Esther 4:14 applies equally in the life of Jacobson.

Any number of important questions could be asked relative not only to Israel's 60th anniversary, but to her future. Questions that are seldom addressed in Sunday School classes, Sunday morning sermons, home Bible studies, etc. Consider only a couple.

Why is the modern church so neutral toward Israel at best, and even virulently anti-Israel at worse? It is somewhat difficult to say this, but most in the modern church just do not give a rip about Jews. The vapors of satanically-inspired anti-Semitism have drifted up from the pit of hell and have permeated the camp of the saints. A profound lack of biblical knowledge has left multitudes of minds open to just about any deception that comes along. Most Christians have no idea what the New Testament says about Israel (specifically Romans 9-11) much less what the ancient Hebrew prophets said!

As a result most Christians typically resort to the very weak, but commonly accepted by-line, "Well, everybody knows the facts of the matter — that God washed His hands of the Jews when they rejected and killed Christ, and of course, the church has now taken their place." The next time you hear that statement, kindly ask exactly and specifically what facts they are basing their conclusion upon. Then watch for their response. They will either stammer while searching for a credible source, or become quite miffed that you would dare ask such a question.

Another fair question has to do with the reason God has allowed the reestablishment of Israel. Consider first what is not the reason. That is, Israel does not deserve God's blessings in any form or fashion. They are not always good people thus making them worthy of God's blessings. They are presently in rebellion against God and His Christ. As a nation they believe their survival is because of their own military power and technology. They see no need of God in their affairs of state. Most in Israel today are either agnostics or atheists with their last religious prime minister being Menachem Begin in 1983. So why did God allow the reestablishment of the nation?

Because He said He would do it (Ezekiel 37). Because He made an unconditional promise to Abraham and the Patriarchs (Genesis 15; Galatians 3:17, 18). Because the honor of His name is associated with the promise (Ezekiel 36).). Because of all the unconditional promises God made to them in Jeremiah

30 and 31. The list could go on, but the thrust is that God said He will do it and He will. The old adage that says, "God said it. I believe it. That settles it." is hog-wash! God said He will do it, and that settles it whether someone believes it or not!

Every major leader in the Moslem Arab world stands in opposition to Israel. They reject the Bible as the Word of God, thus they reject the warnings of Genesis 12:3, Joel 3:1, 2, etc. (Interestingly, many who call themselves fervent Christians also reject those same warnings.) At this very moment the late Yasser Arafat, the bloodiest terrorist of the 20th century, knows the truth along with Hitler, Stalin, Amin al-Husayni the late Grand Mufti of Jerusalem and all the rest who relished the flowing of Jewish blood. Soon Ahmadinejad and all his Hezbollah consorts along with Abbas and all the others will also come to know the truth. And they will regret for all eternity their anti-Semitism and the lies they believed and perpetuated.

Further, the UN, that impotent financial parasite that exists solely for its own perpetuity, stands against Israel. In short, though most would not say it directly, the world in general would like to see Israel go away. Except for the hand of God overruling in men's affairs that would indeed happen. In fact, a no-holes-barred effort will be put into motion at the middle part of the Seven Year Tribulation period with its culmination described in Zechariah 14 and Revelation 19.

We can go to sleep with these facts in mind: Jews will continue to exit the Gentile world and return to their land, Israel will not be destroyed and those who go against Israel by forcing her to give away her land "for peace" will be severely punished by God (America take note!). The last 60 years of Israel's existence is only the beginning, and for those of us who grimace at the thought all I can say is we should get used to it, for as God was in the burning bush, so is He in that nation. DLM

Chapter 17

This Present Fear

~ ~ ~ ~ ~

Illegal drugs, super-intrusive technology, fluctuating oil prices, high unemployment, loss of health insurance, asteroids, killer calderas, Islam, AIDS, etc. People are living in fear, and to not see this is to live in a coma. What, we ask, is happening to our world? Is such fear a part of the times in which we live? Is there an end to this, and if so, what is it? Most everyone can see what is happening — the problem is they just don't know where it is going.

Though the numbers are rapidly falling, many of our citizens remember happier days, like those of the 1950s. Though there was always the Cold War, bomb shelters and rock & roll, yet most people lived in serenity and peace. After all, Russia was a long way off and at least some parents still thought Hank Williams might eventually trump Elvis the Pelvis. The Statler Brothers sang of such times in their nostalgic songs like "Do You Remember These" and "Carry Me Back". Life was much simpler back then not because there were no troubles, but because most everybody believed the threats were only temporary and a happy ending was always in sight. Not only are those days gone, but hardly anyone with any level of discernment sees a happy ending on the horizon anymore. Except, of course, Christians.

Scarcely any family can say it has not been touched at least to some degree by the drug curse. Fifty years ago it was all about cigarettes and beer, but those crutches have been shifted to a lesser category of concern and have been replaced by every kind of deadly chemical one can imagine. Poison, readily available to all, is now smoked, snorted, swallowed, injected, topically assimilated and otherwise introduced into the body. And each one has its own deadly outcome. No longer able to shield their kids from unsavory influences, parents are often suspect of their kid's peer group, and even their cell calls and text messages because drug use is woven into almost every seam of their modern sub-culture's fabric. The result is parents feel helpless and resign themselves to the false sense of security that comes with, "If he/she can just make it out of college everything will be OK." For these reasons people fear for their children and grandchildren.

People living in the American Southwest understand their civilian police forces and local Nation Guard units are totally incapable of stopping and containing a mass cross-border assault by drug cartels whose intent would be terror and hostage-taking for ransom. The truth is not "if", but "when" such an event might happen. Fear at our borders.

Property crimes are escalating in the areas of burglary and robbery. Daylight break-ins are very common, and even those houses with warnings about alarm systems are often hit. This is often done using the smash-and-grab method. The thugs are in and out in less than three minutes with guns, TVs, etc., as loot. Don't be fooled by TV advertisements implying the immediate response of security monitoring companies. That is not reality. Fear for property and possessions.

A gun dealer said recently the purchase of hand-guns went up dramatically after the November election because, "...people are afraid of Obama's anti-gun sentiment." Law abiding citizens view strangling restrictions on the purchase and possession of weapons and re-loading equipment along with the serializing of ammunition as hostile government annulment of the U.S. Constitution. They know that when citizens are disarmed they not only become immediate victims of totalitarianism, but also the prey of thieves, rapists, murderers and the rest of society's dregs. They consider depending on 911 in personal assault and crimes-against-property emergencies as government-sponsored dial-a-prayer. Fact or fiction? Take a good look at current events and you decide for yourself. Fear for personal safety.

Now that oil prices are down, at least temporarily, some people no longer even have expendable income to enjoy the respite. Loss of employment means not only a downsizing of life-style, but the loss of health insurance and retirement plans. This kind of thing is quite traumatic for people in middle-age who are depending on their stock investments to assist their pension plans. No time to recoup. Fear for retirement.

And speaking of oil there is no end to the terrible scenarios that can be put on the table if Iran launches an offensive against Israel (which they have said they will do in time), or if some military or naval commander in or near the Straits of Hormuz has to pull a trigger. Oil prices will be impacted if a strong hurricane smashes into gulf coast refineries, or if a pipeline is sabotaged – there is almost no end to the possibilities. Fear of substantial business failures and further economic downturns.

Earthquakes. Most everyone understands that the explosive power of a large magnitude earthquake is unimaginable. What is now on the minds of many people is the high risk of such an event actually happening in some area like New Madrid, MO or southern California. Food, water, and fuel supplies will be cut off. Air, rail and highway transport will stop. Civil unrest will erupt. In short, an unprecedented Pandora's Box of serious problems will instantly descend upon a major portion of the United States. Fear of nature and resulting chaos.

The Islamic attack on America in 2001 left an impact that is very much present today. People are not so willing to trust the world's diplomats because they know diplomacy very often fails and when it does many people die. And with today's weapons being sold to the highest bidder, both conventional and WMDs, the casualty list could be astronomical.

The result of an NBC attack (nuclear, chemical or biological as such attacks used to be labeled) is beyond belief. No American president has ever had to warn our citizens that such an attack was in progress. No board of Joint Chiefs has ever had to defend the U.S. against such an attack already in motion. Nobody has ever seen the effect of an NBC attack upon millions of people. The truth of the matter is the trenches of WW1, the Hiroshima bomb and Saddam's attack upon the Kurds can no longer be considered realistic examples of a large and coordinated NBC attack on a major metropolitan area. The carnage would be beyond the pall. Fear of global war and immense suffering.

AIDS has not been cured, and unfortunately it is politically incorrect to advocate AIDS prevention in the realistic form of heterosexual monogamous marriage and avoidance of illegal drug use. Some of the most effective drugs used to fight common staff infections are no longer as effective as they once were. Even hospitals can be sources of illness and death. *Nationally, a study released in October 2007 found that an estimated 94,360 patients annually in the United States develop an invasive infection and nearly one in five, or 18,650, die as a result. The number of deaths exceeds those caused by HIV/AIDS or homicides each year* (www.klinespecter.com/ hospital_infections cited 10 Feb 09). Fear of uncontrollable pathogens. Fear that places of refuge could no longer adequately and safely provide relief.

Politically things are not fairing much better. It seems a growing number of people are now fearful of loosing their God-given rights of free speech, freedom of the press and the right to bear arms among others. Social engineers have for years condescendingly labeled such fears as unfounded and reactionary, but current trends no longer allow such distrust of government to be ignored. Many people are reconsidering the old adage: an unarmed citizenry is a government's dream, whereas an armed citizenry is a government's nightmare. Fear of political repression and the annulment of the right to private ownership and control of property.

Modern technology, like any tool, can be profitable or regrettable. Along with the benefit of being connected worldwide and thus able to do business overseas while driving one's car, there is the fact that virtually nothing is private any longer. With technology government can know people's spending habits, their bank accounts, who they talk to, what they talk about, what they own and how much, their travel habits, the value of their inheritance, etc. And there is absolutely nothing anyone can do about it. What was once "none of anybody's business" is now information available to almost everyone, and especially the government.

This is producing a somewhat different kind of fear. A fear that the gathering of information will be used in the future to tax and control people in a way never seen before in history. Some people sense a heavy and foreboding spirit of stifling repression on the near horizon. And they feel helpless to stop it. Do you suppose this might have something to do with absolute population control as seen in Revelation 13:16, 17?

Well, what about it? Can all of this be evaluated in a clear and concise manner? Yes. Maybe the best way to look at these matters is to, in a manner of speaking, place them on some sort of easily viewed schematic, tape it to a wall then step back and make an unemotional, unbiased, realistic evaluation of the whole scenario. Oh, and one more thing. You have to put it all in biblical perspective because then, and only then, can the truth be known. Leave out what God has said and every secular theory will invariably lead to a dead-end. Omit scripture and every single conclusion about the days in which we live and their end will be flat-out wrong.

The truth is this world is not going to get better in any major category. Don't look for President Obama to be able to solve anything permanently. Ahmadinejad will not suddenly decide to be nice to Israel. The Taliban will not stop beheading hostages. Oil will not stay cheap. The so-called Palestinians will not make peace with Israel, two-state solution or no two-state solution. The world will not see permanent better times economically. Illegal and deadly drugs will still be in demand. Political oppression will always be government's tool of choice in controlling people. No part of the country will be immune from danger. There will be more dread diseases than cures. And, as time goes on the list of things to bring concern and fear will grow longer than the world's list of peace-assuring guarantees.

Of course, Christians will not be here to see the consummation of such events. We, like the rest of the world, see what is going on and how terrible things are. The difference, however, is we know something more — how it will end. Thus, we do not fear as those who have no understanding of where these events are leading. We know where they end and what to expect. And, we know of our imminent deliverance.

The world, including many professing Christians, is fearful. Even some Christians are wringing their hands, losing sleep, accumulating arterial cholesterol and otherwise destroying their witness to this dying world of the Blessed Hope (Titus 2:11-13) because they do not really understand where all this is going and how it will end. They do not understand because they refuse to accept the plain sense of Bible prophecy. Sad.

For Christians all pain and despair will end with the rapture of the church. For those left behind the trials, misery and sufferings of today are not even in the same league with the torment and affliction of those coming days. The best way to say it, I suppose, is what is coming is incapable of being clearly described. Yep, it is going to be that bad.

While the spiritual/allegorical means of Bible interpretation is often the cause of dismay, anxiety and fear regarding current and prospective events, the literal, plain-sense interpretation of Bible prophecy is the great cure. Allegory, you see, is void of peace. Indeed, we are living in the darkening shadow of Revelation 6, but we do not panic, become alarmed or distressed. Because we take God for His literal word we not only understand what is happening and why, but we know how it will end. God, our Father, does not use cryptic codes, theo-babble and non-sensical allegory to give us information He wants us to know and understand. He speaks plainly, and we are to simply believe it. Let there be no present fear in the heart of any Christian. DLM

Chapter 18

The Earth Post Rapture

~ ~ ~ ~ ~

For some reason deeply embedded in the mind of Almighty
God planet earth was chosen as the battle ground against Satan.
Sin originated in heaven when Satan attempted to take the
throne of God (Isaiah 14; Ezekiel 28), but that is not where it
will end. Of course, he was defeated in that battle, but the war
was far from being over. Though Satan was unable to capture
the Throne Room of Heaven he did not quit. Rebellion had
been born, and God could not stop until it had been destroyed.
The initial skirmish had been won, but the war for complete and
permanent sovereignty was still to be fought. And it would be
fought on earth.

I believe it quite possible that God created the world as we
know it as recorded in Genesis at some point after Satan's rebellion. No one has any idea regarding the eras of time that
were involved in these matters. Time as we know it did not
then exist, and God has chosen to not give us information regarding these events. However, we do know some things. In a
manner of speaking the great eye of God scanned the vast emptiness and, for whatever reason, He chose to create a small planet where this whole sin/rebellion/redemption issue would be
played out. Earth is just a speck of cosmic dust in the grand
panorama of things, but a speck of dust more important than all

others because of the battle being waged here.

At the beginning the earth was pristine in every way. Adam and Eve were perfect and did not ask for, nor even think of anything that might be lacking. Until, that is, one day when the evil one approached Eve while she was alone and put an idea into her mind that had heretofore never been considered. In essence, he suggested to her that if she would simply act in rebellion against God she would become a goddess herself. After all, it was not a big deal — just eating some fruit, and besides, the benefit would overshadow any retribution God might deal out to her. So she did it, and so did Adam. Satan won that battle, and the rest is history.

Fast forward to this present moment. Judging from what we see when we place current events over the template of the Bible, it looks like the grand finale is nearly here. The next event on the schedule is the rapture of the church when every Christian (in the true sense of the word) will be taken from this planet so quickly the time sequence will be impossible to measure. Soon after, the terrible events of the tribulation will begin to happen, and those events will come to an end with the last great battle on earth. The run-up to Armageddon will begin soon after the rapture, and the earth as billions have known it for millennia will be forever changed. This is called the tribulation period, and Jesus said nobody would survive if the time would not be limited.

The tribulation period, also known as the 70th week of Daniel chapter 9, will be a time of unprecedented horror for those left behind. Anti-Christ will appear, catastrophic geological changes will occur, oceans and seas will be ruined, the world economy will collapse, God's righteous judgment will be poured out and untold multitudes will die from war, famine, disease and an animal world gone berserk. Revelation 6-19 describes those events.

The disappearance of the church in itself will throw this planet into a level of chaos that is impossible to imagine at this point. Nobody knows how many people will be taken. Millions? Hundreds of millions, or billions? We simply do not know. But, this we do know: it will put this world on its head in more ways than one.

The disappearance of multitudes will impact different countries in different ways, but the net result will be felt worldwide. In countries where relatively few people are Christians the infrastructure will see little immediate change. Saudi Arabia and other Moslem countries are strongly anti-God by official policy. That means there are few Christians there, and hardly any of those are in critical government, military and industrial positions. The same can be said about China and North Korea.

Though America is basically in the toilet spiritually speaking, yet there are many Christians scattered about in most every field, even possibly some in Congress (tongue-in-cheek). Our military has many believers, and at least some of those are in the senior NCO and general officer ranks. When the rapture occurs it is quite possible our Armed Forces will go to a very high state of readiness, not knowing what happened and what to expect. If a number of commanders in critical positions are taken several things will happen.

First, the chain of command will be broken. To civilians that probably means little, but to those familiar with threat-response-protocol it could mean a lot. Intelligence-gathering will be affected, and the loss of some top-level analysts will seriously hinder the government's ability to accurately sort out what has happened. This will cause panic, and panicky people are apt to go off half-cocked. Strategic and tactical communications will probably be affected. Whatever information that will be available will go up and down the chain of command with a lot of distortion. Indecision, doubt and a whole lot of second-guessing will most probably be running amuck — a dangerous thing at any time, and especially so then.

The stock markets of the world will probably drop like a rock with investors pulling out of everything while they try to figure out what has become valuable or worthless in a matter of just a few hours or less. Even when drastic swings in the global markets can be explained logically, financial panic still has a way of making everything go to pieces. This, however, will be compounded at the rapture for at least two reasons. Multitudes will suddenly disappear before the very eyes of throngs of people, some of whom will be big cogs in big wheels in big industry. Piles of clothes along with jewelry, dental fillings, pace-makers, etc. will lie rumpled in the exact place where just a nano-second before an associate was standing. In less than an eye-blink they will be gone. And secondly, 99% of those who see it will not have a clue as to what just happened in plain view, and why. The fallout from this inexplicable event will be further complicated by those religious leaders left behind who will lie and use deception to answer the questions multitudes will ask.

Civil authority and emergency response systems will be in shambles. Several days ago a disgruntled customer at a fast-food place called 911 because the burger-joint had run out of his favorite meal—chicken nuggets! We are amused at this person whom we might label as a dunce, but we must not miss the lesson to be learned here. What do you think that same person, and tens of millions of others, will do when the rapture happens? Communications systems will be overloaded in people's frantic efforts to find missing family members. Put into the equation the number of Christians working in public safety professions who will be removed and it is easy to see how the chaos will be compounded.

And we cannot leave out the criminal element. They, of course, will be left behind and it won't take them very long to see this situation can be used to their advantage. They will not care about what happened or why. They will only see opportunity, and with emergency response agencies operating at minimum at best the sewer-dregs of society will embark on a campaign of civil terror few alive today have seen. It will come down to sur-

vival of the strongest and smartest. And if a socialistic government has disarmed the populace it will be like shooting fish in a
barrel for the criminal element.

It could be that burglary will become less common because
criminals will not even try to avoid personal contact with their
victims with the net result being an increase in armed robbery
and aggravated battery. Murder will probably be committed
with an air of casualness (as is often the case presently), and
sexual assault could be on the scale of that which happened in
chaotic eastern Germany as the Red Army swept through in the
spring of 1945.

And, we must not forget what will happen to the Jews. The
Holocaust will be just a little second-string warm-up compared
to the post-rapture situation. The anti-Christ will hate Jews
with a seething passion that would be the envy of Hitler and
Ahmadinejad. Anti-Semitism will eventually become public
policy, and people will jump on the band-wagon with vim and
vigor. Why? Because all anti-Semitism is satanic in nature.
Second, it will be to everyone's economic, social and professional advantage to cooperate with the anti-Christ in his program of genocide. Third, he will use the same tactic Hitler used
in 1933 — point the finger of blame at the Jews for everybody's
pain and suffering. Everybody, except those sheep nations of
Matthew 25, will be quite pleased to involve themselves in the
new world fuhrer's brilliant plan to finally rid the planet of the
real reason for the world's problems. "If we could just get rid
of all Jews", they will think, "then everything will be ok."

In Nazi Europe synagogues were burned, and at times scores of
Jews were herded into the buildings to be burned alive as the
flaming structures fell upon them. Multitudes were shot while
standing at the edge of open pits so their bodies would fall into
the hole — that way there was no valuable time wasted drag-
ging corpses, you see.

Diseases will take their toll. Today a simple infection can be simply treated by a simple anti-biotic with little time lost and no real inconvenience. However, when the drug is not available due to disasters like earthquakes, volcanoes, floods, tornadoes, civil chaos, etc., then those simple infections can result in death. That which is today very simple will then become both complex and deadly.

And one other thing about the post-rapture earth to consider is the mark of the beast. This mark must be taken by everyone in order to buy or sell. When people take his mark they automatically sign their own admission papers to a burning hell for eternity (Revelation 14:9-11). And they will do so with full knowledge of what they are doing, for the gospel will be declared to the post-rapture earth by the two witnesses, the 144,000 Jewish evangelists and an angelic herald.

Put simply, what this means is people who need to buy anything for health and survival — anything at all — must have the mark. How many will be willing to allow themselves or their loved ones to die for lack of food, medicine, etc., in order to not take the mark? What about a parent with a dying child that is born in that time? Further, the head of the apostate church will force everyone to take the mark or have their heads cut off, like it or not (Revelation 13:16).

We must understand something very clearly: the post-rapture earth will not be different simply because Christians will be gone. It will be more than just a missing-persons kind of thing. People will suffer in unspeakable ways and will die horrible deaths from natural disasters, disease, war, starvation, aggressive animals and crime. While in college years ago a friend told me he wanted to stay behind at the rapture in order to preserve law and order "down here". I could not decide which word best described him, ignorant or foolish — or maybe both.

Let there be no misunderstanding. The church has always experienced tribulation, and will continue to do so until Jesus returns for her. However, she will not be given over to the situation above. Maranatha, come, Lord Jesus! DLM

Chapter 19

Psychic Blunder

~ ~ ~ ~ ~

Though it is really no joking matter, listening to people call into programs featuring psychics can be hilarious. Most people can easily see how the caller is manipulated in the conversation. Psychics are charlatans; simple frauds who prey on the ignorance of some people. Some say there actually is some kind of strange power with some of them. If so, we can believe with full assurance it is demonic and not divine.

FoxNews.com reported how a famous psychic was seen as a fraud just a few days ago. When the Sago mine tragedy occurred Sylvia Browne, a TV psychic, was on George Noory's live syndicated radio show. She was making comments on the tragedy about how everyone survived but one man. She said she knew they would be found alive and directly said so.

In just moments, however, while still broadcasting live, the news report came that all but one were dead. Browne was now in a pickle and didn't know what to say or do. Squirming, she said, "I don't' think there's anyone alive, maybe one. How crazy for them to report that they were alive when there weren't! I just don't think they are alive." At that point she cleared her throat and what followed was a "deafening pause" according to the Fox News report. Noory tried to help Browne out of the hole she was digging for herself, but the more she talked the deeper it became. That she is a fake was obvious to the whole world!

Human nature has a natural and dangerous inclination toward most anything that is out of the ordinary. Satan, the father of all liars, exploits this interest by using seemingly mystical phenomena to capture and channel a person's fascination to a point where scriptural discernment is quickly replaced by some kind of transcendent influence. It seems one of the immediate goals of such demonic activity is to bring the person to a point where they begin to believe they are privy to some sort of cryptic information. Pride soon becomes inescapable and the duped victim develops a condescending attitude toward anyone who might be in disagreement, especially family members and close friends.

God has warned us to not get involved with evil. The occult and related activities are not simply child's play. Satan is the greatest fraud the world has ever known and will use anyone who chooses to dally around with that sort of stuff. There is no such thing as toys when it comes to the occult; not Ouija boards, Tarot cards, etc. Christians are warned to stay away from the occult, astrology, pseudo-Christian groups and any other such activity.

Actually, the bottom line is quite simple: the activity itself is demonic and those who participate are deceived.

Chapter 20

Netanyahu, Ahmadinejad & Obama

~ ~ ~ ~ ~

The new Israeli Prime Minister, Benjamin Netanyahu, recently granted an interview with Dave Eberhart of Newsmax. Interesting interview.

In essence Netanyahu gave notice to America and the world that somebody has to do something with Iran and its virulently anti-Semitic president, Mahmoud Ahmadinejad. US President Obama said though it was "unacceptable" for Iran to have nuclear weapons, he wants to try diplomacy first. So, if Secretary of State Hillary Clinton fails in the diplomatic effort, does President Obama have what it will take to morph his words into action in the face of the maddening Islamic world? Interesting question.

Look at some contrasts between the three men. Netanyahu is an MIT graduate, has a graduate degree, was a member of the Sayeret Matkal, an elite special forces unit of the Israeli Defense Forces whose main responsibility is counter-terrorism and intelligence gathering and has years of experience in Middle Eastern politics.

Ahmadinejad led the uprising against the US Embassy in Tehran in 1979 when 52 Americans were held hostage for 444 days, has a PhD in civil engineering, is intimately familiar with Middle East politics and hates Israel and America with a passion.

Obama, with a virtually unknown past, has a law degree from Harvard, was a US Senator for a few months, was a community organizer and knows essentially nothing about international politics, Middle East politics in particular and especially how they affect world stability or instability. Interesting contrast.

Maybe this is something to think about. Must we wonder as to why America is not specifically seen in Ezekiel 38 and 39 as a deterrence to Russia and Iran as they assault Israel? Can we examine the future as recorded in the Bible and get perhaps just a glimpse as to the direction Obama might lead the US regarding her relationship with Israel?

Specific answers to specific questions regarding these matters are difficult to offer in light of the fact we do not have every piece of the puzzle in front of us. However, it seems evident Obama will not be seen as a staunch ally of Israel, the only trustworthy friend our country has in the turbulent Middle East. This automatically causes him to default to being in opposition to God, and what is in opposition to God looses His blessing. Very interesting scenario.

Chapter 21

Job's Question

~ ~ ~ ~ ~

A number of years ago Dr. J. Vernon McGee told the story of an atheist in Hanover, Germany who decided, even if he were wrong, that his body would never be resurrected for any reason. He left instructions that his casket was to be entombed in tons of concrete, covered with granite and secured with steel bands. Inscribed on the tomb were the following words, *This tomb is purchased for eternity. It shall never be opened.* Amusing how God has a sense of humor. You see, a poplar seed fell behind one of the straps and grew through the years. When this tomb was found just before WWII it had been broken open by the tree. God might have been saying, "You can't even seal a tomb in this life; how can you know anything at all about death on your own?"

Each of us has some idea about death, the afterlife and resurrection. In casual conversation we often use the phrase, "Well, I believe..." Dr. Spiros Zodiates relates the story of a group of people who happened to be discussing various issues at a party. Someone said something about a type of physical malady and was corrected by a man who was a physician. He said the malady was complicated and that people should only listen to physicians when discussing such matters.

Later the matter of the resurrection came up and this same physician spoke long and authoritatively about it. The problem was he did not have a clue as to what he was talking about. When corrected and asked where he got his ideas he became defensive and said that his views are what he believed based upon his own thinking. It seems he thought that was supposed to impress someone.

The man from Hanover and the physician are no different from most people. They believe what they want to believe about death and resurrection without regard to the truth. They rest in their self-appointed expertise and draw conclusions based upon their secular educations, experiences and, more significantly, their personal wishes. Eternity itself is not long enough to fully regret such foolishness.

When a man falls short of, or goes beyond God's revelation about death and resurrection he is performing guesswork and is stepping out into thin air. Books have been written about what some people call near-death-experiences, and it is interesting that most people going through those things "return" as different people. Not that they have necessarily seen the truth, however. They are just different in some ways. Some become more caring, more generous or more loving toward their families. Such changes are indeed good, but their dramatic cause might have absolutely nothing to do with the truth. Humans have a tendency to associate all things they see as supernatural with God — a very dangerous position to take!

Job asked, *When a man dies, will he live again?"* (Job 14:14). The human mind has never asked a more pertinent question. To get the answer to that question one must go far beyond speculation, science, politics, etc. He must go to the truth; that is, what God has said about the matter. Anything and everything else is quite simply guesswork, and quite often it is not very accurate at that.

Why is this so? Because all of man's many achievements fall

short of answering the question. As someone once said, man can get to the door of death where he can knock, but there is no answer — except from God.

What can a non-Christian say to someone who has lost a loved one? A President can present the Medal of Honor to a young widow, but if said president is not a Christian about the only words he can offer are, "Thank you for your sacrifice. Be strong." A close friend or even a relative can only say, "I love you." A physician can only say "I did the best I could. I am so sorry." But, all of that is so empty, so hollow, and so impotent. Why? Because those words, no matter how sincere, come from a human perspective and cannot even come close to answering the real question, *Will my loved one live again?*

Easter is nearly upon us. It does not have all the commercial appeal as Christmas, but it is my favorite celebration because it is God's answer to Job's question, not man's answer. Forget rabbits, eggs and all the other stuff that goes with Easter. Such is fun for kids, but is not even remotely associated with life after death. Sadly, in their efforts to make a connection between those icons and the resurrection I have heard some preachers make some very long stretches in their sermons. People leave churches like that with their question still unanswered — *if a man dies, will he live again?*

Easter answers a resounding "Yes!" to Job's inquiry. We will indeed live after death! For those who base their belief system upon their own spindly and flawed considerations, they will live again in a place called hell. They will have bodies, will feel torment, will have memory and will forever regret their pride and self-imposed importance (Luke 16:19ff though referring there to Hades instead of hell).

For those who are Christians (narrowly defined, by the way — Matthew 7:13-24) we will be forever in the presence of Jesus and our saved loved ones, will never know pain, sorrow or death again, and will have bodies like that of our resurrected

Lord (Philippians 3:20,21). That answers the question!

Jesus said to Martha, Lazarus' grieving sister, "I am the resurrection and the life; he who believes in Me shall live even if he dies and everyone who lives and believes in Me shall never die." (John 11:25, 26). That is the truth; we need go no farther. All that can be said about the matter is there. There is no human-inspired assurance anywhere and under any name that can even approach the comfort of those words. Not just because they are inherently comforting, but because God in human flesh said them; the same One who was dead and who is now alive, even this very moment sitting at the right hand of God soon to come for His church.

The key to whether this is comforting for someone personally is found in the final sentence of verse 26, "Do you believe this?" Whether the truth of the Easter resurrection applies to you depends upon how you answer that question.

Get beyond the shallow musings presented on satellite TV programs where false extra-biblical "gospels" are presented for your consideration. Forget so-called recently discovered ancient documents and previously hidden secret codes. Do not waste your time on such things for they are all false and offer nothing of real value. Such is mere human speculation and presumption — not worth one cent or one second.

So, if a man dies will he live again? You bet! Jesus is the living and unquestionable proof of that. With that said the only remaining question is, *where*? DLM

Chapter 22

Mahmoud Abbas & Peace in the Middle East

~ ~ ~ ~ ~

Israel is about 8,000 miles from the east coast of the United States, and what happens there is often ignored by most American citizens. Except for a few minutes on the nightly news about homicide bombings committed by Moslems against Israeli civilians and soldiers there is actually very little that the average American knows about what is going on in that part of the world. And because the world media in general hate the Jewish state a lot of what people hear is from a very tilted and biased viewpoint. For example, the Moslem murderers of innocent men, women and children are often portrayed as "freedom fighters" while the Israeli responses in defense are seen as acts of "military aggression".

The core of the fight that is going on presently is the question of the so-called Palestinian State. There never has been a Palestinian state, and until the 1960s no body was really concerned about it. However, in an effort to destroy the State of Israel the Arabs began demanding that part of Israel be given to them as a homeland and that the city of Jerusalem be given to them as their capital. The truth, though, is the world media are refusing to admit the Arabs already have a state and its name is Jordan.

Before his death Yasser Arafat was the president of this imaginary state he called Palestine, and after his death the Arabs chose a successor named Mahmoud Abbas. It is clear many in the United States and Europe are placing a lot of confidence in the recent election of Mahmoud Abbas as the new Palestinian Authority president. So great is this confidence that Abbas' election was hailed by governments around the world as the first great step in bringing peace to the Middle East because, they tout, Abbas is a political "moderate".

Mahmoud Abbas, also known as Abu Mazen, was born in Safad in the mountains of Galilee (what is now northern Israel) on March 26, 1935. When Israel became a state again in 1948 Abbas went to Syria and taught in an elementary school. He later earned a law degree from Damascus University and a Ph.D. in history from the Oriental College in Moscow. He spent time as a bureaucrat in Qatar and became involved with radical Arabs. He co-founded Fatah along with Yasser Arafat and finally was elected as the PLO Executive Committee's Secretary General in 1996 which placed him in the position of Arafat's deputy.

Abbas is seen by many as being devoted to a peaceful solution to the Israeli-Palestinian conflict. For many years he has maintained contact with liberals in the Israeli government and was the PLO representative that signed the Oslo Peace Accord with Israel in September, 1993. Because of this many Arabs consider him to be too conciliatory toward Israel. However, there are some radical and anti-Semitic skeletons in his closet that the world is ignoring. Unfortunately even many in Israel are ignoring this wolf that is disguised in sheep's clothing.

First is the matter of his being the co-founder of Fatah, that large terrorist faction that is part of the PLO. In 1965 he and Yasser Arafat put this group together in order to intimidate by any means anyone who might question the Arab demand for more of Israel. You see, as a result of politics the Arabs have already gotten about two-thirds of the land promised to the Jews. A large chunk of the land east of the Jordan River was promised to the Jews along with the land west of the Jordan promised to the Jews along with the land west of the Jordan River. In fact, the *Times* of London on 19 September 1919 called this land for the Jews "a good military frontier".

But, a certain Arab leader named Abdullah ibn-Hussein got some noisy tribesmen together and took over the part east of the Jordan River. So, in order to appease and keep them quiet the British, in 1923 took the area known today as Jordan from the Jews and gave it to the Arabs. Thus at the very start the Jews lost the majority of the land promised to them. Fatah never mentions this event and continues to demand another Arab state be carved out of what little is left of Israel. Neither does anyone else mention it.

Additionally, Fatah played a key role in the recent election by restricting the amount of news coverage received by the three candidates running against Abbas. As you might guess, the Palestinian media are controlled by Fatah. The *New York Sun* on December 31, 2004 quoted one Arab voter as saying, "People are afraid to be seen even reading their literature." The PA is the largest Arab employer in Judea and Samaria (known to the world as the West Bank), and the message Arab voters received from the PA leaders is that if anyone votes for the three challengers they will lose their job or they can be assured they will never be hired by the PA. That was not a small, insignificant threat. No wonder Abbas garnered nearly 70% of the vote!

Mahmoud Abbas wrote a book in 1983 called, "The Other Side: The Secret Relationship Between Nazism and the Zionist Movement" where he denied the Holocaust even happened. Further, he played a key role in the September, 1972 massacre of Israeli athletes at the Munich Olympic games by providing the financing for the attack; an attack carried out, by the way, by Arafat's Fatah faction of the PLO. [1]

Abbas, like Arafat before him, has never genuinely renounced his terrorist connections. Just one day after the U.S. State Department took $23.5 million from the pockets of American tax-payers and gave it to the Palestinian Authority (December 29, 2004) Abbas went to Jenin and campaigned with members of the terrorist al-Aksa Martyrs Brigade. A picture was taken of him riding on the shoulders of one of the world's bloodiest terrorists, Zakaria Zubeidi. When asked about the picture, especially after giving the PA millions of American tax-payer dollars, Secretary of State Colin Powell admitted the photo was "disturbing", but said, "I don't think it reflects Mr. Abbas' overall approach to governing." [2] Mr. Powell seems to be living in a twilight zone.

In the analysis it seems clear that Abbas' supposed "opposition" to terrorism is all politics; a move to ingratiate him to the western world thus hiding the way things really are. Consider, for example, Jeff Jacoby's statement that Abbas is portraying himself as a moderate and that he, "...has no *moral* problem with blowing up buses and cafes, he simply thinks such methods are, for now, counterproductive." [3]

Yes, he is called a "moderate" by most everyone. However, don't count on the accuracy of that label. He is a terrorist — Arafat wore a uniform and Abbas wears a suit. As one commentator put it, "The talk may change, but the symbols and intent remains the same. And the Mainstream Media is just lapping it up, not bothering to do any in-depth questioning of what they're willingly propagating down the wire." [4]

All of this is common knowledge, so why are people buying into Abbas and his program? Especially, why are many Israeli's supporting Abbas? It would seem they, of all people, would question every aspect of Abbas and his plan. Yet, they do not. Former Israeli Prime Minister and current leader of the Labor Party Shimon Peres recently said about Abbas, "I think very highly about him and even more so about the way he was elected." Obviously some in the Israeli government are willingly being duped. So, why is this happening?

The answer to that question is multi-faceted, but there are at least two answers that need to be considered presently. First, many in the Israeli government are humanists. That is, they believe in the ultimate goodness of man and they believe that changes in the environment will lead to changes in the human heart. They believe if they give enough of their land to the Arabs in negotiations for peace (thus changing the environment) then the Arabs will have a change in heart and will no longer want to destroy Israel. The result, they say, will be peace at last. This, of course, is absolute nonsense because no amount of environmental change in the form of land-for-peace will change the hearts of terrorists. Yet, when a person disavows the sovereignty and work of God in the human heart then this kind of claptrap is about the only thing they can fall back on.

Secondly, the people of Israel and many of her leaders want peace so badly they will listen to just about anyone who will guarantee cessation of hostilities. They simply want to be able to enjoy what we enjoy in our country. To not be unduly fearful about going to bed at night, riding a bus or driving to work the next morning, sending their children to school, enjoying a meal in a public restaurant with their family, traveling on a public highway, visiting their holy places, etc. Multitudes of Jews have been killed while going about their everyday business including a six-month old baby who was targeted and shot through the head by a Moslem sniper while in her stroller. Something, by the way, that hardly made the evening news at the beginning of this current intifada.

Israelis are bone-tired of spilled Jewish blood and the heavy, ever-present sense of uncertainty that fills each day of their lives. They just want to live a life of peace and to be left alone. A noble desire, but Mahmoud Abbas is certainly not the one to fulfill this dream. He is a deceiver and any trust the Jews place in his intentions will be rewarded with only more death and heartache. Unfortunately that is the way it will be until Jesus Christ replaces the final deceiver — the anti-Christ. DLM

Chapter 23

Getting Rid of God—Then What?

~ ~ ~ ~ ~

Looking back upon the last several years of American history
consider what the following people have in common: David
Hager, Jerry Tacker, J. Leon Holmes, Michael McConnell,
Charles Pickering and Priscilla Owen. If you said they are people who were nominated for appointments to government pan-
els and the judiciary you would be correct.

Consider another list: Senators Dick Durbin, Dianne Feinstein
and Charles Schumer. What these people have in common is
they are all liberal senators who did everything in their power to
block the appointments of the people on the first list. Why did
they do this? Was it because the nominees were either unquali-
fied or criminals? Not at all, for they all had impeccable credentials with stellar records.

You see if these people had been liberal, pro-abortion nominees
with a secular/multi-cultural worldview they would have been
confirmed with no argument. But, they had a problem; they all
have a strong Christian worldview, and that is something that is
absolutely unacceptable to the anti-God crowd.   In fact, Sen.
Schumer said of Holmes, "This man is an embarrassment to be
nominated...This guy is so far off the deep end...I do not know
why this man was nominated. What he thinks is so bad." [1] Did

you get that last sentence? That is, Schumer thinks the Christian worldview is something that is bad for America. How so? Probably because Christians believe in godliness, righteousness, accountability and the existence of moral absolutes, the direct opposite of the secularist agenda.

Anti-Godism is no longer something the secular sect tries to keep secret. Those who oppose any vestige of Christianity in the public specter (and anywhere else, for that matter) are now coming out of their closets with bold declarations and a marketing strategy that is being swallowed hook, line and sinker by a docile and ignorant American public. There is no doubt the anti-God crowd is growing in both influence and noise-making.

All you have to do is consider secular society's view of Christmas. Never before has such an effort been raised to take Christ out of Christmas as we are seeing today. Oh, there have always been those who have worked against the spiritual aspect of the holiday season, but never before on this level. Public school students have been told they cannot have Christmas parties and cannot sing Christmas songs. It is acceptable to sing about reindeer, snowmen and Santa Claus, but kids can no longer sing about Jesus and His birth. The parties students are allowed to have can have no reference to Jesus' birth. You see, the politically correct reference today is to call Christmas the Winter Holiday, or some other such "neutral" name.

However, the ACLU, atheists and others so inclined to be anti-Christian are strangely inconsistent in their demand to have no Christian references during any part of the year in public bodies, whether schools, agencies, etc. The Jewish menorah is allowed to be displayed during Hanukkah in many schools and government work places, and, of all things, the Islamic crescent moon is allowed to be displayed during Ramadan.

The reason for this inconsistency? According to government bureaucrats and the ACLU the menorah and the crescent moon are not religious symbols, but are rather cultural symbols. This is absolutely incredulous. But, what is even more incredulous is that many people are accepting this cockamamie explanation with very little protest! The ACLU likes to say they work to protect the rights of all Americans. I think this is a very pristine and pure form of hogwash. Can anyone verify how many times the ACLU has filed suit against a government agency or private company on behalf of a Christian who has experienced discrimination because of his faith?

The fact of the matter is that the anti-God crowd is growing in number and influence. Christians are being branded as reactionary and dangerous. In some places such as Europe it is said to be in vogue to be anti-Christian. [2] It clearly seems the same mind-set is alive and well in our own country. For instance, a Christian fraternity at the University of North Carolina at Chapel Hill, Alpha Iota Omega, was forced by the school to close because it discriminated against students who had other religious beliefs. [3] What about those Moslem campus groups who discriminate against Christians who would like to join and become leaders? Has UNC or any other school shut down those Moslem groups? I think not.

So, what will be the outcome of all this anti-Christian stuff? Well, first God is going to give them exactly what they want — a world without Christians, and it might happen a lot sooner than some think. When Jesus takes His church off this planet the world will be just as the ACLU and other anti-God people want. That is, they will be rid of people who have a Christian worldview, who believe in absolutes, who believe God is still God and has not divested Himself of His sovereignty and who believe homosexuality, abortion and other such abominations are wrong. When the rapture happens some will no doubt know what has happened and will be quite distressed. But, for most people it will be a time of gladness after the initial shock of millions of people disappearing has worn off.

But, there is more to it than simply being free from Christians. What follows the rapture is not something the anti-God rogue associations will celebrate with joy. Hell will break loose on earth to such a degree that people will try to kill themselves in order to escape the suffering, but will be unable to do so by Providential design.

Once the church is removed God is going to inflict rebellious humanity with a degree of wrath that is absolutely unprecedented. We must understand, however, this time of tribulation will have several purposes. First, it will be a time when God will deal with the Jewish people in order to bring them to their knees before their Messiah Jesus. It will also be a time interlaced with God's grace, for though the church will be gone yet the invitation to eternal life will still be open, though it will cost people their lives. The 144,000 Jewish evangelists will be at work (Revelation 7) along with the two witnesses (Revelation 11) and the angel who will preach the eternal gospel to those on the earth (Revelation 14). It will also be a time when God will avenge the blood of His saints and will severely punish those anti-God forces which have demeaned, ridiculed, persecuted and otherwise terribly mistreated those who were Jesus' own; those whose only crime was to be Christian.

But, it is the unmitigated suffering that will take center stage during this time. As Jesus opens the scroll with the seven seals the wrath of God begins. As an example of what will happen once the world is rid of Christians consider the events associated with the breaking of the first four seals, commonly called, "The Four Horsemen of the Apocalypse" (Revelation 6). The first rider is on a white horse. He is the anti-Christ, the false messiah, the great counterfeit, the world's last great leader and the one who hates Jesus with a terrible passion. He will have a plan and will offer the world "peace", something the whole world will buy into without reservation. Little do they know what they are actually buying.

The second rider is on the red horse. This rider takes away any "peace" the first rider might have temporarily brought and ushers in a time of bloodshed that is unimaginable. War is a growing problem and there is no end in sight, humanly speaking. Forget the United Nations; it is not only an impotent body, but is a perverse, crooked, leftist, Israel-hating impotent body.

An interesting thought in Revelation 6:4 is the great sword the rider carries. In Greek the word refers to a dagger, the weapon of an assassin. This indicates it will be a time of bloodshed that is not limited to warfare, but includes civil turmoil when old scores will be settled and private vengeances carried out. It will be a time of civil butchery that cannot be contained. How can this be? Remember that Paul called the anti-Christ *the man of lawlessness...the son of destruction* (2 Thessalonians 2:3). His agenda will be limited to power and worship of himself. Human life will be of no concern. You see, when God is kicked out, lawlessness enters the vacuum.

The third rider enters the scene on a black horse — that of famine. War, earthquakes, climate change, etc. all have their impact on the world's food supply. With a shortage of food comes rising prices and rationing; it all goes hand-in-hand. A quart of wheat is the least amount of nourishment one man needs for one day. If that is all a man can get in one day and if there are others in his house who depend upon him for the provision of food and sustenance then someone is going to get very hungry. Barley is animal food, something only slaves ate during hard times. And even that will not be in great supply.

Interestingly, though, the oil and wine will not be in short supply. Expositors have variously applied that text, but many attribute oil and wine to the luxuries of life. Can you imagine that? Starving to death while staring at a big-screen TV! Starvation on this level will not take very long to occur. It is also interesting to note that ten thousand people starve to death daily in our world while about 15% of edible food in America goes into garbage cans with some dogs in America getting more protein than most of the world's population. This is not an indictment against America's affluence, it is simply an example of the unparalleled change that will suddenly happen in those days in this, the "land of plenty".

The fourth rider comes into view riding an ashen horse. In the Greek the color is a pale green like that of a rotting corpse. Death comes by way of the sword, famine, disease and wild beasts. Surely, we might think, the carnage caused by the other riders is enough, but it is not. Just when the anti-God earth-dwellers think it might be over it becomes even worse with even more death and suffering. And instead of repenting before God feeble man shakes his puny fist in the face of the awesome God (Revelation 9:20, 21). Twenty-five percent of all humans left after the rapture will die at just this point, and the wrath of God is nowhere near being over.

Okay. So the world does not want God and His people around anymore. Well, one day God will give this anti-God world exactly what it has been wanting. He will take the church off this planet, He will pull back His hand of mercy and grace and what will result will be a time of pain, misery, terror and death that is nothing less that incomprehensible.

Is this something that, if it even happens at all, is in the distant future? I do not think so. Remember something about Bible prophecy — great prophetic events have a way of casting their shadows before them. We are living in the darkening shadow of the coming tribulation even this moment. How can we know this? There are many reasons, not the least of which is the reestablishment of Israel in their ancient homeland.

But, there is something else: the level of anti-God and anti-Christian rhetoric is being cranked up at almost an exponential rate. The change even in the last two years is very evident, not just in America, but in the entire world. That this world-wide anti-God attitude coincides with what is happening in Europe and the Middle East is by no means a coincidence. Things are happening and they are happening at an increasing rate. We wait and we work while we wait. DLM

End notes

1) David Limbaugh, "Anti-Christian Litmus Test". *Townhall.com*, 6 August 2003. Cited 17 December 2004. Online: http://www.townhall.com/columnists/davidlimbaugh/printdl20030806.shtml

2) Marion Baillot, "Buttiglione Cites 'Anti-Christian' Fad", *The Washington Times*. 11 December 2004. Cited 17 December 2004. Online: http://washingtontimes.com/world/20041211-114117-7361r.htm

3) George Archibald, "Anti-Christian Charges Probed". *The Washington Times*. 18 August 2004. Cited 17 December 2004. Online: http://washingtontimes.com/national/20040818-114636-5163.htm

Chapter 24

Hardened Hearts in the Tribulation

~ ~ ~ ~ ~

What Jesus revealed to the Apostle John in the book of Revelation is a scenario that goes beyond anything any script writer could ever imagine. The pain and suffering that will come upon people during the time of the tribulation is too horrible to imagine, and that is one reason why John often used the word "like" to describe what he was seeing. Quite simply, he had seen no precedent for what Jesus was showing him.

Chapter nine is an interesting chapter, not only because of the dramatic events that are described there, but also because of three verses that have to do with the hearts of men during those times. The time frame is, of course, the 7 year tribulation period, and the main events of the chapter are the sounding of the fifth and sixth trumpets. But, these particular verses go beyond mere events to reveal the deep degree of godlessness, spiritual decay and hopelessness that will exist in the hearts of many who are left behind at the rapture.

When the fifth trumpet will sound creatures that John described as locusts will come out of the bottomless pit and their only goal will be to torment sinful men in a most painful way. For five months they will inflict a level of suffering that is extraordinary — they will not kill people, but will sting them with some sort of stinger that will produce pain and suffering as when a scorpion stings a person. The context indicates there will be no escape from these creatures and no relief from the terrible suffering they will inflict. At each turn people will be stung, perhaps many times per day. In bed, in the shower, while driving, at work...no escape and no relief. This will go on for five months. So, the first verse to note is verse six which is indicative of how hopelessly unbearable the pain will be, *And in those days men will seek death and will not find it; and they will long to die and death flees from them* (Revelation 9:6).

The other two verses that capture our attention regarding these matters are verses 20 and 21, and these aptly show just how hardened the human heart can, and will become. *And the rest of mankind, who were not killed by these plagues, did not repent of the works of their hands, so as not to worship demons, and the idols of gold and of silver and of brass and of stone and of wood, which can neither see nor hear nor walk; and they did not repent of their murders nor of their sorceries nor of their immorality nor of their thefts* (Revelation 9:20, 21).

While reading these verses it might seem at first that it is inexplicable that the people going through those horrors will refuse to repent before God and cast themselves upon His mercy. Yet, adamantly refusing to repent inspite of knowing much suffering is the consequence of the rejection of God's standard is, in fact, today's norm. And that is exactly what they will do in that day. Even from a purely secular level hardened hearts have a way of suppressing logic and common sense. Consider STDs and AIDS, for example.

Further, it seems that in light of all that is happening around them, people will clearly see that this horrible series of events is nothing less than miraculous; that is, it is out of the ordinary and must of necessity be by the hand of God. Actually, the people who will go through this will indeed know this is of God! Revelation 16:21 clarifies this matter of their knowing from whom the plagues are coming, *And huge hailstones, about one hundred pounds each, came down from heaven upon men; and men blasphemed God because of the plague of the hail, because its plague was extremely severe* (emphasis mine). Yes, people will know who is sending these plagues and why. But, they will not be able to kill themselves in an attempt to escape their suffering while continuing in their refusal to repent.

There is a big question about all this. If they will know who is doing all this and that the reason is their rebellion toward God, then why will they not repent of their sin and turn to Him? After all, the cause-and-effect will be so obvious! The answer can be found in something that might not be so obvious to the casual reader of the Bible. Miracles in the absence of faith have only one result: they tend to harden the human heart.

On the surface such a statement seems almost incredible, but that does not detract from the truth of it. Consider the story in Mark 6:1-6. In that text Jesus was in His hometown of Nazareth teaching in the synagogue. The people listening to Him had known Him all His life, and they just could not believe this hometown-boy was indeed the Messiah. Verse five says, *He could do no miracle there except that He laid His hands upon a few sick people and healed them.* It did not matter that Jesus performed miracles in their presence; the majority of His fellow citizens simply refused to believe in spite of those obvious miracles. And the reason they refused to believe? They had no faith, and the result was that their hearts were hardened. This has always been, is now and always will be the case. Likewise, the people in Revelation 9:18ff will not repent because their lack of faith will harden their hearts, and the presence of the miraculous will change nothing.

One of the things that makes this passage so sobering is the probability that many people alive today will be among those very same people described in that text. Could this really be? Yes. The return of Jesus for His church, commonly called the rapture, is imminent. Soon after the rapture Israel will sign a treaty with a world ruler whose biblical name is anti-Christ, and the signing of this document will signal the beginning of the tribulation period, the period in which these events will take place.

It is of great importance to understand that the events of Revelation are not necessarily relegated to some time in the distant future. And there are at least two reasons for this. First, there is no Bible prophecy that must be fulfilled before the taking of the church. It could happen at any moment. Second, the world stage is ready with the main players (Israel, the European Union, the United Nations, the World Council of Churches, and others) already on stage and moving quickly to their positions for the opening scene. A number of people alive today will, in my opinion, be those we read about in these passages. Many will die from the plagues described beginning in chapter 6, but many will still be alive to experience first-hand the sting of the locust-creatures in chapter 9 and will be there to shake their puny fists in the face of God.

The inability to die by some means is something that is associated only with the locust-creature plague. In verse 15, when the sixth angel sounds his trumpet, 33% of those still alive will die. Some will believe that death will bring relief from their suffering. Not so! Death will only move a person from the torment of the earthly plagues to the fiery torment of those who die separated from Jesus Christ. This same false sense of relief associated with death is common even today. But, the truth of the matter is this: no matter the kind or degree of a person's suffering, death will not bring relief if that same person is not a blood -bought disciple of our Lord.

There are those who think that the judgments of Revelation are just too terrible for God to pour out. They believe God is love and that He could never do these things even to rebellious humanity. True, God is love, but love is only one facet of God's character. God is also a God of justice, and a just God cannot allow sin to go unpunished. Jesus died to take upon Himself the punishment due to every human being. This means the same

God who righteously demands payment for sin also provided that payment on the cross. Redemption is free to all who will make Jesus both Master and Savior. What some folks seem to forget is that He will not be our Savior without also being our Master. Jesus is not simply a "fire escape" saving people from hell and then allowing them to live in rebellion to Him. And that is the problem with the people in Revelation 9. They would dearly love to escape the torment of the tribulation, but their decision to not place their faith in Jesus prevents them from wanting Him as Lord of their lives — the direct result of hardened hearts.

God is indeed righteous in His dealing with rebellious humanity in this way. Take a look at Revelation 16:5, 6, *And I heard the angel of the waters saying, Righteous are You, who are and who were, O Holy One, because You judged these things; for they poured out the blood of saints and prophets, and You have given them blood to drink. They deserve it.* Twice in that chapter, verses 9 and 11, John records that rebellious humanity will actually blaspheme God because of their sufferings, but they simply will not repent! As late as chapter 14:6 John says God will send an angel to proclaim the gospel message to those who are still in rebellion against Him and to warn them to not worship anti-Christ and take his mark. Most, however, will not listen.

No, these judgments are not the random and capricious actions of a God who has lost His temper at humanity. God is without question righteous in pouring out His wrath upon a race of people immersed in their sin and in their hatred for Him. It is nothing less than amazing that He will even offer grace and mercy to all who will accept it during this time, but He will. And faithless and hardened hearts will simply not respond to that amazing offer of pardon.

That many will be saved during the tribulation is a fact (Revelation 7). However, one would be very wise to not consider this as an option to exercise after the rapture. 2 Thessalonians 2:1-12 says that God will allow those who did not love the truth to be deceived in their belief system during that time. Further, if a person chooses to not serve God presently when it is easy (at least in our country), what makes that person believe they will do so when this decision will cost them their life? Also, our next heart-beat is not promised, and once a person dies (often suddenly with no warning) that person no longer has opportunity to repent and accept God's mercy. Death is the end of every opportunity, and there is no appeal.

The tribulation. Jesus said it will be a time of unprecedented world trouble, and the sketch we have in Revelation does not fully present the total horror that will be played out during those years. Our only hope is in the coming of Jesus for His church. It could happen at any moment, and it is that very moment we love and pray for so fervently. Maranatha! DLM

Chapter 25

Hurricane Katrina

~ ~ ~ ~ ~

In the last several weeks much has been said and written about Hurricane Katrina. Some say the storm was just another storm and that no real biblical significance should be associated with it, while others say it definitely was a form of judgment from God. I can find no middle ground; either it was allowed or sent by God for a purpose, or it was not.

I believe the storm was indeed something God used in an attempt to get the attention of not only the Gulf Coast region with all its ills but the entire nation, and I also believe any spiritual message intended to be associated with it has mostly been ignored.

A Heavy Hitter

Prior to the 2005 hurricane season FEMA listed the three most potentially cataclysmic events that could impact America. First was a powerful earthquake along the California coast, next was another horrific attack by Moslems and third on the list was a category five hurricane hitting New Orleans. Though Katrina was a category four storm, its devastation was something far beyond expectations.

The impact a hurricane has at landfall is dependent upon several factors including storm strength, population density, land elevation, previous rainfall, etc. Katrina weaved several of these factors together to form a very formidable storm when it made landfall on August 29 at 6:10AM with sustained winds of 145 mph and higher gusts. The pressure was 27.108 inches (918 mbar) with a storm surge of 30 feet at Biloxi, the highest to ever hit the U.S. Many historic buildings were destroyed that day. The cost is estimated to approach $200 billion which is over twice that of Andrew, Fifi, Hugo and Charley combined.

New Orleans is below sea level with many commercial and residential areas constructed on land that has been back-filled with millions of yards of dirt. The land is so mushy that pilings had to be driven into the ground in many places to prevent poles supporting TV antennas from sinking.

One of the greatest reasons for the number of deaths is that many people refused to leave this lowland. Those who had no personal vehicles were offered transportation, but such help was refused by many. Thus the death toll was high; nearly 1300 total with over 1000 in Louisiana alone.

Katrina — Punishment as opposed to Judgment

But, there is more to the storm and what it left in its wake than mere meteorology and physical damage. For those who take the time to look more closely it is clear that Katrina, Rita, the recent earthquakes out west, the Asian tsunami, the AIDS epidemic and a host of other heretofore common occurrences are not, in fact, simply common. In the minds of many these are signs...signs that point glaringly at an imminent event that is too wonderful for words for Christians, and likewise has no precedent in its horror and evil for those who will be left behind. Commonly called the rapture of the church, it is when Jesus will remove His church from planet earth followed by a seven year period of sustained judgment upon this earth and all who rejected His offer of grace.

If all this sounds too unbelievable, implausible, preposterous and bizarre to imagine then you have pretty well sized it all up. But, it is true. And Katrina is just the latest in God's warnings about what is on the near horizon. Warnings most ignore.

Though it might seem trivial, there is an important difference between punishment and judgment. Punishment is a warning, an act of mercy which should cause one to recognize his sin and turn from it thus putting himself in a position for God's blessings. Judgment, on the other hand, is an act of justice wherein a person gets what he deserves; the time of mercy is over. Moses warned Pharaoh nine times to let the Israelites go. Each time Pharaoh changed his mind and kept the Hebrews in slavery with the result being that God, knowing he would not relent, judged both Pharaoh and his country. The tenth event was not mere punishment — it was a judgment. The first-born of both man and beast, including Pharaoh's family, died on the night of the Passover.

You see, God became fed-up with Pharaoh's rebellious heart and sent an event that had all Egypt weeping and wailing at dawn. Not an act of mercy in a form of punishment, but only the falling shoe of judgment.

Is this the way things are in the U.S.? Have our people pushed God to the point that He is sending punishments in order that we might repent of our national sin thus bringing us back to the place where He can bless us? Though it is not politically correct in some circles to say so (and not religiously correct in other circles), yet it is very clear to me that this is indeed the case. Take a look at what might be some reasons.

America's Track Record

When our country was founded our forefathers built it upon biblical principles. I know humanists cringe and get migraines each time they hear this, but it is a fact. Examine our founding documents. Read the Mayflower Compact. Consider what great men like Patrick Henry and James Madison wrote and said. The Bible was a reading primer in those days.

But, unfortunately all that is now obsolete. The godless secularists say America is now liberated from those early Christian principles and can now bask in the warm light of freedom and self-indulgence. They say we are much better off today because we are now free to kill babies before they are born, free to gamble away our family's sustenance, free to live together without marriage, free to practice homosexual perversion, free to do all sorts of things that would have been unthinkable even 50 years ago.

America dismissed prayer from government schools in 1963. It is interesting to note that when teachers and students could pray there was no fear in our schools. Today it is unlawful for teachers and students to mention God, Jesus, Easter and even Christmas in schools. No cross, empty tomb, carols, manger or wisemen; no nothing that has anything to do with the person of Jesus. God was told to leave. He did. And He was replaced with fear, horror and moral and educational degradation.

America's Middle East Policy

But, there is another public policy that brings God's chastisement and that is our official policy toward Israel. As a matter of policy President Bush forced Ariel Sharon to give up part of Israel to the Arabs for their "state", and the giving is not nearly over. Secretary of State Condoleezza Rice said it must really hurt for Israel to have to do this, but it just had to be done for the sake of peace, and she said a lot more must be given up in the near future, too.

She told Israel not to worry, though. She said when the Palestinians have their own state and become involved in civic affairs like building playgrounds and filling in potholes they will give up their time-honored practice of murdering Jews. And just think, some people actually think her evaluation is a brilliant piece of diplomatic insight! And all that was only after President Clinton put the weight of our country behind the foolish and disastrous Oslo Accords.

Consider carefully what is God's Middle East Policy. First, He said Israel is His land (Isaiah 14:25; Jeremiah 2:7; Ezekiel 36:5, etc.). Second, He said He gave it to Abraham's descendants through his only legitimate son Isaac (Genesis 21:12; 22:2, 12). Third, God pronounced a blessing on those who bless the Jews and a curse upon those who curse them (Genesis 12:3). Fourthly, God said He would judge any nation that had a hand in dividing up His land (Joel 3:2). And as a result of years of misdirected American foreign policy we find ourselves cruising on the very borderline between God's present punishment and ultimate judgment. A blind man can see this. Is there any real question that the natural and political events we have suffered in our country of late are divorced from the will of God?

The promises of blessing along with the threats of judgment upon any nation that puts itself at odds with God's foreign policy regarding Israel are as sound and valid today as they were on the day they were made. They simply need to be believed without regard to human logic.

For example, Joshua made a decision to circumcise the men of war as they entered Canaan to do battle though doing so was an extremely foolish decision militarily speaking. Obviously the warriors would be unable to defend their nation while they were healing (Joshua 5:1ff). But, Joshua did do it, and he did so because that is exactly what God said to do. You see, he was more concerned with obedience to God than he was about maintaining a good defensive perimeter. Has this eternal principle grown too difficult for the self-professing Christians working in Washington to understand?

New Orleans and the Gulf Coast

One of the reasons most people refuse to see Katrina as a form of punishment from God is the death of so many innocent people and the destruction and hardship many good and upstanding people had to endure. Consider several thoughts in this regard.

The suffering of the innocent is the result of sin in the world, a very heart-breaking yet very simple premise. Herod killed little children in Bethlehem. Thirty-six innocent men died as a result of Achan's sin. Innocent people die when a driver gets drunk and crosses a centerline. The common refrain is that the death of innocent people is not fair. True, but life in general is not fair. The crucifixion of Jesus was the most unfair thing to have ever happened in human history. The innocent often suffer as a result of the sin of a few or even only one; millions suffered and died as a result of Hitler, and whole families can suffer as a result of an abusive husband and father.

Gambling was rampant along the gulf coast. And gambling, like prostitution, is not a victimless crime. Politicians and many citizens point to the millions gambling brings in to the public coffers—about $500,000 per day in Louisiana. But, it is not without serious problems. It hurts families. Just look around at the children who suffer because of the lottery and video poker. Gambling causes people to focus on materialism which in turn causes people to forget God. Faith in God is replaced by faith in a $100 million lotto ticket; that is, people think money will do a better job at taking care of them than God. In gambling many people must lose a lot in order for one person to win a little. Remember: the house never loses!! The bottom line is that games of chance are in direct opposition to godly principles of living.

New Orleans is known for its debauchery and depravity. In fact, the city wears this label as a badge of honor. Mardi Gras is all about living with the morals of a pot-licker hound until midnight of Ash Wednesday then at the sound of the tolling bell it suddenly becomes sin. The idea is "live like you want" then go get absolution the next day. Women are thrown worthless trinkets and beads from passing floats if they flash their breasts for

for the men doing the throwing. Video cameras are constantly filming the activities and some are eventually posted on the internet much to the chagrin of some of those women.

Perhaps the most infamous celebration in New Orleans is called Southern Decadence where homosexuals come from all points of the compass to take part in parades, parties and public activities that would make a demon blush. Not only has the last three mayors endorsed this celebration, but Mayor Ray Nagin (of Katrina fame who said he was a target for execution by the CIA) proclaimed a couple years ago, "There is no place like this on earth! Southern Decadence XXXII is an exciting event. We welcome you and know that you can anticipate great food, great music and great times in New Orleans." (worldnetdaily.com) John d'Addario said in "Southern Decadence 2005: A How-To Guide", "Southern Decadence may be most famous for the displays of naked flesh which characterize the event...While police have started to crack down on public lewdness and pressure from a local *crackpot conservative religious organization* has caused the five-day festival to become a little more sedate than it was in years past, the atmosphere of Southern Decadence has stayed true to its name and public displays of sexuality are pretty much everywhere you look." (emphasis mine)

A local preacher made the effort to video some of those "public displays of sexuality" as they occurred on public streets, and sent copies to members of the city council. It was ignored. You see, SD brings in lots of money to the city, and the city fathers and mothers believe it is OK to put up with a little perversion if it increases revenue. Surely God understands.

Looting, murder and rape were common after Katrina. Of course, in New Orleans murder is common most all the time. The looting was obvious with large numbers of people caught on tape, and the items they were most often stealing were not "necessities", unless you consider drugs, jewelry, electronic equipment, etc. necessities during an emergency. Rape is not often reported at any time and a number of police officers said perhaps many of the rapes were not reported for obvious reasons such as the loss of phone service and the scarcity of police.

Most people have no idea how much tax-free cash money can be made selling pharmaceutical-grade narcotics on the street immediately after such a disaster. That is one reason they were killing each other in order to be the first to loot a drug store.

Space will not allow referencing some of the comments about Katrina by celebrities, atheists, homosexuals and others who believe their opinion counts for more than yours or mine. But, I will mention Billy Graham. Mr. Graham said some good things about God and His love and mercy, but I could not find one single reference from him about God's clear warnings regarding debauchery.

Inevitable Punishment

If there is indeed a connection between this catastrophic storm and America's spiritual depravity, and if God is indeed trying to get our attention, then our country is coming in line for even more problems because most people, even some Christians, are not listening. In fact, some are even upset and angry with those who believe God might indeed be using such cataclysmic events to get our attention. They do not want to hear that message because it does not fit with their unbiblical notion of who God is and how He works in the lives of people and nations. Is it true, as they so strongly believe, that God got rid of the wrath aspect of His nature when the first words of the New Testament were written?

In the late 1930s some in the U.S. military warned Washington about the imperialist intentions of the Japanese Empire. The warnings were ignored and classified as the railings of warmongers. In those days foolish men like Neville Chamberlain ignored the obvious and placed their hope for the world in the milk of human kindness. In the 1950s the politically and socially elite of our country were busy brushing aside the warnings about communist and socialist influences; warnings that were coming from those they deemed unsophisticated and reactionary. The consequences of past naivety are now clear each time we note the cost in terms of both dollars and lives. Are we seeing that same variety of God-mocking attitude today?

Call it what you will, when all the facts are laid out it seems without question God is working through such natural disasters to bring us around spiritually. Though we see mercy in Katrina in that it could have been a category five and could have gone straight up the mouth of the Mississippi, yet very few acknowledge that. And as far as bringing us around morally and spiritually as a city, state or nation — it won't happen.

Unfortunately the damage is done and we will never be what we once were or what we could be. We still see the patience and mercy of God with such punishments, but it is not known when He will say "Enough!" and allow our alienation from Him to have its natural end — destruction. One thing is for sure. Such disasters along with unstoppable pathogens, Islamic hatred and economic failures will not go away. Rather, it seems we will see an increase both in intensity and number of these and other calamities. And the sad part is most people are listlessly saying "peace and safety" with sudden destruction looming (1 Thessalonians 5:3). It is only a matter of time. DLM

Chapter 26

Islam—A Trojan Horse

~ ~ ~ ~ ~

The mythical story of the Trojan Horse serves as a very good illustration of how something that looks benign can be, in fact, very destructive. The Greeks attacked the city of Troy, and for ten years had no success at breaching the city walls. Finally, they retreated and left a giant wooden horse outside the gates. Inside the horse were armed Greek soldiers waiting for the opportunity to be pulled inside the walls of the city. Convinced the Greeks had given up and gone home, the Trojans pulled the horse inside the city thinking it was some kind of peace offering from the retreating Greeks. The entire city celebrated in a drunken uproar. After the celebrating Trojans had passed out from the alcohol, the Greeks unsealed the door and climbed out of the horse. They quickly killed the sentries and opened the gates. The entire Greek army came in and took the city killing the men and boys and taking the women and girls as slaves. By dawn everyone in Troy was either dead or in bondage.

I believe Islam can be considered such a Trojan Horse because many Americans, leaders and constituencies alike, can not see insidious nature of this religion. The President of the United States and the Secretary of State refer to Islam as "one of the world's great religions", and essentially give it moral and spiritual equivalence with Christianity. After 9-11 Mr. Bush was very accommodating to the Islamic clerics in the US and constantly reiterated that this was not a war against Islam, but rather a war against terror. Last November, while speaking to a Muslim group in the US, Mr. Powell implied very strongly that Jerry Falwell, Pat Robertson, Franklin Graham, and other such evangelical Christians are bigots because these men issued warnings against the impact and influence of the bloody religion of Islam. Is it not reasonable to ask if perhaps Mr. Bush and Mr. Powell have lost their faculties of discernment?

I want to make several observations about this situation and the possible consequences. First, what we are involved in is indeed a war against Islam. To confirm this simply read the Koran. The Islamic clerics calling for "death to the Great Satan (the US)" are not heretics preaching fiery sermons which are outside the parameters of Koranic teaching.

Terror is not the enemy; it is a tool of the enemy. While in Vietnam we did not fight against AK 47 rifles and punji stakes. We fought against the Viet Cong and the North Vietnamese Army which generally consisted of men wholly dedicated to both Marxism, and to the destruction of any opposing force. AK 47 rifles and punji stakes were merely two of their weapons.

Terror is a tool of the Islamic religion that is used to gain their objective, and that objective is to subjugate as much of the world as possible. To believe we can live as a free people and be at peace with Islam is to put ourselves in the same boat of self-deception as British Prime Minister Neville Chamberlain who, after leaving a September 30, 1938 meeting with Adolph Hitler said, "I believe it is peace for our time." The rest is history.

What is the danger? Islam is a Trojan Horse, but it is no longer waiting at the gates to be pulled inside; it is inside already! We must not think the religion of Islam will not change America. It already has. Fifty years ago no American was worried about the influence of Eastern religions, including Islam. Today the influence is all around us.

How has this happened? I think it is quite simple: America now worships the god of "tolerance", and this has opened the door to a terrible enemy whose aim is to impose upon everyone the religion of Allah. This is the stated aim of Islam's own clerics. So, why do political leaders insist these clerics do not mean what they say? Most probably because they want peace very badly and think such tolerance is the only way it will be achieved. They are deceived.

What can happen? Look at what has already happened with the influence of Islam in cities like Detroit where the Moslem community rushed into the streets to celebrate the Islamic attack on the morning of 9-11. Think about the oil dollars Islamic countries have invested in the American stock market, which in itself presents a very real economic danger.

We think of the effort of Moslems to get possession of a nuclear device of some type, and detonate it in a major city, a power-grid nexus, a critical river-control structure, etc. But terrorism is not limited to weapons of mass destruction. It can come in another form: that of technology. Islamists can use computer programs called "Trojan Horses" (something similar to computer viruses and worms) that can confuse, disrupt, manipulate, modify or even destroy oil/gas delivery systems, power grids, 911 systems, government agencies and private industry. Such programs are called "Trojan Horses" because they appear benign and even beneficial, but are nothing less than devastating. They typically infect PCs in the form of gift offers such as, "You have just won a Caribbean cruise." Mainframe attacks can be different, but just as effective.

God has warned His people such things would become prevalent during what is called the "end times". To identify what we are seeing as genuine signs of the end times is no knee-jerk reaction by ignorant people looking for the anti-Christ behind every bush. Such world-wide pandemonium is no longer science fiction; it is now a very real possibility. Many thought 9-11 would be the much-needed wake-up call for Christians and for unbelievers, but it has not had a permanent effect. Life goes on with mundane routine with little or no thought to the imminent return of Jesus for His church, which is both our blessed hope (Titus 2:13) and the purifying factor in our lives (1 John 3:2,3).

But, there is a positive side to these matters. The threat of war, the rise of Islam, the falling stock market, etc. all have people (including some Christians) wringing their hands in anxious anticipation of the forth-coming dooms day. But, for the believer who is listening for the trumpet such things are not so much warning signs as they are welcoming signs, for it is those very signs that announce the season of our Lord's return. For our children's sake we must be concerned and involved regarding these matters, but we must not be troubled. Jesus did not promise us a smooth and threat-less journey through this life, but He did promise us a safe journey with a certain and glorious end.

The public in general is frightened by what they are seeing. They fear the loss of their jobs, the further deterioration of their retirement funds, a substantial reduction of their affluent standard of living, unprecedented national debt, and a type of war we have never before seen in our country.

Now more than ever people need to see their Christian friends, neighbors, and family members living with a sense of peace and assurance that stands out like a flashing beacon of hope in a black morass of evil and uncertainty. To Christians who love the appearing of Jesus Christ for His church these things are not morbid harbingers of doom and gloom; they are exciting signs that indicate our journey is almost over. DLM

Chapter 27

The Davidic Covenant

~ ~ ~ ~ ~

A study of the biblical covenants can be as detailed as the student would like it to be. This would include an examination of the Hebrew word *berith* which means "to fetter" or "eat with", both of which have the idea of a mutual agreement; or "to allot" which has to do with a gracious settlement of a problem or need. In the New Testament the term is generally associated with a bequest which leaves something to someone by way of a will upon the death of the covenanter. In the context of this article, however, we will consider the term as an agreement between two parties.

The Bible records God's establishment of several covenants including the Edenic, Noachian, Abrahamic, Sinaitic, Levitical, Davidic, the new covenant in Christ, etc. Covenants can be divided into two very basic types: the conditional covenant which requires the fulfillment of certain agreements by both parties, and the unconditional covenant which is a promise one party makes to another without regard to the conduct of the other party. An example of a conditional covenant is the new covenant in Christ whereby God will save sinners contingent upon their accepting Jesus as both Lord and Master. An example of an unconditional covenant is the Noachian, where God promised to never destroy the world again with water, no matter the conduct of His creation,

> *Then God spoke to Noah and to his sons with him, saying, Now behold, I Myself do establish My covenant with you, and with your descendants after you; and with every living creature that is with you, the birds, the cattle, and every beast of the earth with you; of all that comes out of the ark, even every beast of the earth. And I establish My covenant with you; and all flesh shall never again be cut off by the water of the flood, neither shall there again be a flood to destroy the earth."(Genesis 9:8 -11)*

The covenant God made with David is an unconditional covenant. That is, no matter what David did or did not do, God's covenant promises to him and his house were going to be kept (2 Samuel 7:8-16). As David was dying his final thoughts turned to the great promise God made to him years earlier, and he reminded himself that, though he was about to depart this life, the covenant was not only unconditional, but everlasting (2 Samuel 23:1-5). By faith he looked to the distant future when everything God had promised would come to pass through his greatest Son, Jesus the Messiah. The angel Gabriel renewed this promise to Mary (Luke 1:31-33), and James, the half-brother of Jesus, referred to it in Acts 15:15-18 during the Jerusalem conference.

The covenant is found in 2 Samuel 7:8-16...

> *"Now therefore, thus you shall say to My servant David, 'Thus says the Lord of hosts,'I took you from the pasture, from following the sheep, that you should be ruler over My people Israel. And I have been with you wherever you have gone and have cut off all your enemies from before you; and I will make you a great name, like the names of the great men who are on the earth. I will also appoint a place for My people Israel and will plant them, that they may live in their own place and not be*

disturbed again, nor will the wicked afflict them any more as formerly, even from the day that I commanded judges to be over My people Israel; and I will give you rest from all your enemies. The Lord also declares to you that the Lord will make a house for you. When your days are complete and you lie down with your fathers, I will raise up your descendant after you, who will come forth from you, and I will establish his kingdom. He shall build a house for My name, and I will establish the throne of his kingdom forever. I will be a father to him and he will be a son to Me; when he commits iniquity, I will correct him with the rod of men and the strokes of the sons of men, but My loving kindness shall not depart from him, as I took it away from Saul, whom I removed from before you. And your house and your kingdom shall endure before Me forever; your throne shall be established forever.""

That God would do for David what He promised is nothing less than amazing considering David's sin and the terribly dysfunctional family he had. Not only did he commit adultery with Bathsheba, but he killed her husband. And because he was such a poor father his children committed everything from incestuous rape and murder to insurrection. It must be clearly understood God was not pleased with David and his family, and their conduct was not what He desired. And, the truth is they suffered the horrible consequences of their sin without regard to who they were as a family and that God had made a special covenant with their father David. An unconditional covenant cannot void sin's inescapable consequences.

Yet, it is also true God did, and will do, for David what He promised. And this leads to the obvious and glaring question, why?! Was it because David deserved the covenant blessings? No. Did God somehow make a mistake in making the covenant to begin with? Again, the answer is no. Had the Davidic covenant been a conditional covenant based upon David's consistent godly conduct it would have been scrapped long ago. So, the answer must be found elsewhere. And it lies rooted in the character of God Himself.

God will keep the Davidic covenant simply because He said He would. This is not easy for the finite human mind to comprehend, but since when can any mortal fully comprehend the character, mind and will of God? At times what God says and does simply does not conform to what we would call normal or even right. God's promise to never destroy the earth again by water is duly noted each time a rainbow is seen, and the wicked conduct of the human race is not a factor. When Bible students read about the sin and corruption found in the Corinthian church they might wonder how is it possible that God, through Paul, could refer to them as being "...sanctified in Christ Jesus, saints by calling..." as found in 1 Corinthians 1:2. But, He does.

In order to better understand the Davidic covenant one of the first things we must do is get rid of our own view of the way God should institute His plan, and simply allow Him to be God — grace and all. What we sometimes have trouble understanding is that sin is our choice (1 Corinthians 10:13), and grace is His choice (John 3:16). And for that we shall be eternally grateful!

Further, God made and will keep the Davidic covenant because His name is directly associated with it. That God will keep His unconditional promises to His people for the sake of His name has great precedent in the Old Testament as seen in Numbers 14:13-19 and Ezekiel 36:22ff. In both instances God does what He does because His character will not allow Him to give the nations the opportunity to blaspheme His name by saying, "God promised to do something for His people, but in the end was unable to keep His promise." That will never happen!

Well, what does the Davidic covenant, recorded in 2 Samuel 7:8ff, contain? Basically, it can be broken down into four major parts. 1) David will have a great name (vs.# 9); 2) Israel will have her own land (vs.# 10); 3) David will have a dynasty (house) (vs.# 11-15); 4) David's dynasty will be everlasting (vs.# 16).

Should there be any question regarding the interpretation of the Davidic covenant simply look at David's reply to God after Nathan told him what God was going to do. Read carefully vs.# 18-29 where David himself interprets the basic tenets of the covenant. In those words he acknowledges that the complete fulfillment of the covenant promises will be in the distant future, and that God's word is the guarantee. Also note David confirms the uniqueness of Israel through whom God would do great things for Himself and for His land (do not overlook the term *His* land). And, finally David asked God to confirm His word about this covenant for the express purpose of having His name glorified forever.

During Jesus' day the Jewish people well understood the Davidic covenant and its implications. In fact, Gabriel made sure Mary knew her baby would fulfill some aspects of the covenant when he told her Jesus would sit on David's throne (Luke 1:30ff). David's throne has never been, is not today and never will be in heaven. It is in Jerusalem (Jeremiah 22:1-4). Jesus promised the church in Laodicea that those who overcome will "sit down with Me on My throne, as I also overcame and sat down with My Father on His throne" (Revelation 3:21). Two different thrones, two different places, two different times. Jesus is not sitting on the throne of David today, for He is simply seated next to His Father as He works as our Intercessor.

A careful study will show each aspect of the Davidic covenant has applications to the future. Applications such as Jesus reigning from the Davidic dynasty throne, and David himself being resurrected for the purpose of being the chief prince over his own ancient people (Ezekiel 34:23,24; 37:24-28, etc.).

Throughout the history of David's dynasty unfaithfulness and corruption were present, and God warned He would bring judgment for their sin. Jeremiah 22: 1-5 not only shows the throne of David is in Jerusalem, but also issues a warning about the Davidic dynasty becoming desolate for its sin. And, that is exactly what happened. When Zedekiah was deported to Babylon in 586 BC the throne of David was without a Davidic descendant, and has been for almost 2600 years.

But, desolation does not equal destruction. God promised David a descendant for his throne; One who is called the "greater than Solomon", even our Lord Jesus Christ. At the return of Jesus as described in Zechariah 14 and Revelation 19 we will not only witness the greatest coronation the universe has ever known, but we will be participants in all the regal grandeur and glory. Such has God stored up for those whose hope is in Him.

The full implications of the Davidic covenant are awesome beyond imagination, but a problem exists there for some Christians. Unfortunately, many are very unfamiliar with the covenant and related aspects of Bible prophecy, thus they look upon it as some sort of heavenly fantasy that must be spiritually interpreted. This is an inconsistent means of interpretation. On one hand Christians who interpret prophecy in this way believe some aspects of the covenant because they believe in a literal, historical King David, but on the other hand when it comes to promises having to do with the future they suddenly switch to an allegorical interpretation. The problems of inconsistent interpretation, however, can be easily dismissed by simply taking the covenant in its historical and grammatical contexts, and allowing the Bible to interpret itself.

God is a covenant-keeping God, and we are to be covenant-believing people. When those two facts are fused together in our hearts we can rest well without fear of current circumstances or impending events. For the sake of His name and His glory God will do for His people exactly what He said He would do. And that includes King David. Psalm 121. DLM

Chapter 28

The Tragedy of Hopelessness
~ ~ ~ ~ ~

In the early 1970s I read a story about a Korean merchant marine who fell overboard in the Pacific Ocean. He was alone on deck when he went over the railing and no one was around to hear his screams as the huge cargo ship disappeared into the blackness of the most horrible night of his life. He knew when he would be discovered as missing it would be too late for any kind of search much less a rescue. What made matters worse was the fact that he was in a part of the ocean that was not well traveled, since his vessel had gone off course in order to avoid a storm. He knew his predicament. He understood he would either drown, or be torn to shreds by sharks, a thought that chilled his blood to the bone as he began to feel small sea creatures brushing against his legs.

However, God intervened in the natural course of events and he was rescued some time later by a vessel that just happened to be in the area. It was one of those "one-in-a-million shots", so to speak. Though the anticipation and associated anxiety of dying a terrible death at any moment was gut-wrenching enough in itself, yet it was the sense of utter hopelessness that tormented his soul the most.

No hope — nothing rips apart the human psyche and displays

the depths of human emotion like being without hope. Hell does that, too, but only in a much greater way than merely being lost at sea. You see, in hell there is no deliverance; no "one-in-a-million" shots; not even death itself offers relief for one in that place of horror because that person knows, "This is it". He is there for all eternity. Being conscious, feeling pain, having memory and knowing there will never, ever be an escape are all part of hell as Jesus described the place of the lost dead in Luke 16:19ff.

Such is the case with this world. It is on a collision course with destruction and most people do not understand it. Some do not want to understand it. Others understand, but ignore or simply reject the facts. The idea that not thinking about it will, in some way, make life easier is self-deception.

It is somewhat amusing to listen to the human elite deliberate about the course of this world. Though vehemently denied, could it be that at least to some degree, deeply buried in what is the essence of the human heart they understand the hopelessness of the present course of events? For some this could very well be the truth.

Yet, most deny such feelings and publicly insist mankind in itself has all the answers to a secure future. They issue warnings about war, global warming and population increases that will bring famine and disease. They say we must come together as a race and work toward peace and goodwill. They develop plans and cry for multilateral cooperation. They search the solar system, spending incredible sums of money, trying to discover and understand the world's past hoping to find help in securing the world's future. Education, global economic equality, environmental conservation, health-care research and other such efforts make up the key to the world's affluence and longevity according to their wisdom. Foolish, they are.

What can easily be understood, but is rejected, is the fact that we can indeed know the past and even the future. And the reason this knowledge is rejected en masse is because it comes from God. He has told us all about the past and the consequences of humanity's rebellion against our Creator. Additionally, He has given us a broad outline of what is in the future, both for the saved and the lost. All this information, however, is openly despised and hated because the truth about man's history, his present situation and his certain future quite simply pulls back the cover and reveals the naked depravity and utter foolishness of the human heart. And since this does not fit with man's opinion of himself it is flatly dismissed out of hand. A seduced and secularized world demands to know who does God think He is anyway, that He would instruct humanity regarding how to live. The world, in secular thinking, is not helpless or hopeless.

Who among us, if they really looked at this world system objectively, would genuinely want to live life resting with confidence in human discernment and ability? At least the sailor understood the hopelessness of his situation. Obstinate secularists, however, do not have a clue as to the consequences of a world that has disconnected itself from the grasp of God. What a hellish state of affairs is the end of that kind of life!

Thankfully there is something better; something that gives peace and comfort to the frightened and anxious human soul. And that something is called Christian hope. Its source is found in God Himself as demonstrated in the person and work of Jesus Christ. Hope beats secularism hands down every time.

So, what about this thing called Christian hope? Is it just pie-in-the-sky-by-and-by? Does it simply point us to a fantasy world in the hereafter, but has no real impact in this present life? A thousand times, no! The truth is Christian hope is the only thing that is able to satisfactorily fill the characteristic void that exists in the heart of every human being. That void created by man's innate inability to answer the ages old question, "If a man dies, will he live again?" Looking inwardly to answer the question leaves mankind with abject hopelessness.

It does not take very long for an objective critique to clearly show that money and fame cannot do it – look at the elite of Hollywood. Equally obvious is the fact that education cannot do it – look at European intellectualism. Nothing conceived in the mind of humanity, and nothing created by the collective human hand can transform hopelessness into hope. So what, if anything, can do it?

A true story is told of an early 20th century evangelist who was being ridiculed by a humanist professor while speaking to a large crowd of street people in a major Midwestern city. The doctor questioned then ridiculed the evangelist's premise that Jesus gives what can't be found anywhere else — genuine hope. He praised human intellect and told the preacher that Christian hope is groundless; a phantom created by a simple mind's imagination.

The preacher then asked the learned professor to meet him the following day at high noon on the same street corner with 10 people whose lives have been changed for the better by human philosophy. He asked that the professor bring alcoholics, drug addicts, abusers of women and children, prostitutes, gamblers and any such derelicts who had been delivered from addictions, changed into a law-abiding citizens, changed into loving husbands and fathers consistently employed and providing for their families, or any who had been delivered from any other form of dereliction by the power of mere human philosophy. He went on to say he could produce from that very crowd at least 100 such people who had been changed by the gospel of Jesus Christ. The professor didn't show up.

Jack Hollingsworth of Acts 29 Ministries sings a song about a man named Hopeless. The refrain is: "My old name doesn't fit anymore. I lost some friends when I left that town, but now you ought to see who is hanging around. Peace comes over and he doesn't leave. Joy is just like family and I'm not Hopeless anymore...And that is why they call me Hope for short." Jack speaks from experience. He is from a very dysfunctional family. He was an alcoholic living on the street for 20 years. He tried to kill himself six times. He even jumped from the Mississippi River Bridge in Memphis on one attempt and missed the river! Jack, like multitudes of others, can testify to the power of the gospel of Jesus and the rock-solid peace and hope that comes with it.

You see, Christian hope is not only for the age to come. It encapsulates the troubled soul in real optimism right here and now. Christians see around them a sin-sick and rotting world headed for disaster, but we place our heads on our pillows at night in peace knowing that God even has plans for this very world; plans that most people, and even many Christians, do not understand. Bible prophecy clearly tells of a time when Jesus is going to wrest this world from the destructive hand of the enemy and renew it in the form and fashion He originally intended.

The ancient Hebrew prophets wrote of a time when Jesus will smash all rebellion against His sovereignty, will rule with benevolence and righteousness and will bless humanity with a peace that has heretofore been unknown (Isaiah 2; 11; etc.). This will be the time of restoration Peter referred to in his sermon recorded in Acts 3:19-21. Paul also mentions it in Romans 8:18-25. In fact, the song *Joy To The World* is actually not a Christmas song, but refers to this same time. Jesus Christ will accomplish on the face of this very earth what the world can only dream of doing.

The seed of hopelessness was sown in the Garden and soon nurtured when the race was still very young. A division arose between the descendants of Cain and those of Seth. The Cainite society founded a city, invented and developed the arts and business and laid the foundation of a kingdom based upon secularism. Seth's descendants, on the other hand, came together under the hand of God and laid the foundation for God's work on earth. The problem was not the arts and business. The problem was the Cainites chose to perpetuate the motives and methods of their wicked forefather.

Hopelessness. It is a spiritual pathogen that has infected this planet almost since the very beginning. Satan obscures the antidote for this problem by encouraging people to focus upon their own abilities instead of allowing God to be sovereign in their lives.

As was the case with Ahithophel, Judas and many of our own day, suicide is often seen as the only way out for those whose hope is in this world's system. With AIDS, bird flu, Islamic terror, lawlessness, the threat of global war and every other kind of hellish scenario clearly visible on the near horizon there is no wonder people are fearful and without hope. Humanism has failed them and they don't know which way to go. The only way to go is up, but most are so blinded by the fog of despair and deafened by the chorus of self-appointed saviors spouting some form of humanistic psycho-babble that they have become like a deer in the headlights — frozen in place while facing sudden doom.

Ours is a religion of genuine hope. We do not concentrate on the horrible spectacle of this terrestrial life, but rather we remember the words of Jesus, "But when these things begin to take place, straighten up and lift up your heads, because your redemption is drawing near." (Luke 21:28). DLM

Chapter 29

The Message of Daniel 2

~ ~ ~ ~ ~

Any serious student of the Bible will agree that some doctrines are not always so readily understood. That does not mean they are impossible to grasp; it just means they are understood only with prayer and honest study.

Daniel is not a difficult book to understand if it is taken at face value. That is, if the student does not go into it with a bias against miracles and against the plain-sense meaning of scripture. Modern critics say the book was written long after Daniel was alive because it is simply too accurate regarding historical events that were future to his day. This attitude totally incapacitates the Spirit's work as Teacher and the result is a thoroughly skewed, unbiblical conclusion. So, you might want to refresh your memory by rereading at least this chapter before considering the conclusions presented.

The message of chapter two was given by way of a dream to Nebuchadnezzar, king of Babylon (modern Iraq), and it was actually very simple and to the point: though Nebuchadnezzar, the powerful pagan king, had put an end to what might be called the semi-theocracy of the Jews, yet his own kingdom, and all those which will follow him, will eventually be destroyed and replaced by God's pure and perfect theocracy on this very earth.

It might be amusing that this heathen monarch so steeped in idolatry had no problem eventually believing this while most Christians today just can't seem to get it.

After having the dream King Nebuchadnezzar did not understand it. He intuitively knew it was of great importance, and thus the interpretation was of equal importance. Now, the king had a caste of religious advisors he had always used in previous situations, but it seems quite clear he knew in his heart they were frauds. Perhaps he knew the role they played in Babylon was most often for show, and when it came to something as important as this dream he also knew they just could not be counted on. Because of such seriousness, and in order to validate what might be their interpretation, he required them to repeat the dream to him. Of course, this could not be done and they were all consigned to death.

Daniel and his friends were also to die, but the difference between those four young Jewish boys and the others was the fact that they understood they had the sole, living and only real God to talk to about this matter. God revealed the dream to Daniel and, as you know, he recounted the dream to the king and also gave him the interpretation. What a wonderful faith-building story, and most everyone comes away with a sense of awe and amazement each time they read it.

Sadly, however, that is about the end of the story for most Christians. Though they know the details of the dream intimately, yet they somehow fail to grasp the interpretation. Unfortunately, most readers think the bulk of the interpretation is found as it relates to the details of the image itself. Though that is very important, yet to miss the star of the show is to miss the entire message. And, the star of the show is the stone cut out without hands that smashes and puts an end to all the preceding kingdoms. Further, it grows and fills the whole earth (not heaven!), and will endure forever.

If the student fails to grasp this, the entire chapter is left unfinished; it is like looking at a panoramic masterpiece and only seeing part of the scene. We must never miss the fact that in chapter 2:4 through chapter 7:28 God is talking with a specific view of the Gentile world in mind. And this is the door through which the entire world — Jew and Gentile — must enter in order to understand the plan of the ages — that is, God is going to totally destroy every iota of secular human statesmanship and will install His king on His throne in His land and rule with a rod of iron over His earth. Some of the details of how this will be done are discovered as one studies through the Bible, as well as the fact that other details have been kept concealed. But, in its pure essence this is the termination point of the interpretation according to God.

Nothing could be more simple, yet nothing could be of more importance to our own generation. At least one reason so many people are disillusioned by the guarantees of so-called enlightened and educated society, and are so hesitant about a collapsing financial system and are just plain scared by the entire world having gone crazy with certain communists and Moslems rattling sabers while standing next to nuclear triggers, is because they flat-out do not know what is happening to their world around them, and they don't even know where to go for the answers.

What causes even more sadness is the fact many of those same people are Christians. They have bought into the horribly distorted idea that Israel no longer plays a role in God's plan and that the church has now been given the promises God originally made to the nation of Israel. There is no wonder they are fearful!

To be quite honest, if I believed that stuff I would be on the verge of despondency myself, and for several reasons. First, I would be unable to trust God because I would fear He might, on a whim, void the unconditional promises He made to the church like He did those He made to Israel.

Second, I would fear heaven might not be all God said it would be. After all, if He cannot, or will not, bring about ...*the period of restoration of all things about which God spoke by the mouth of His holy prophets from ancient time* (Acts 3:21) then why should I believe He will bring about anything else His holy prophets predicted including what the New Testament says about heaven?

Can we trust Paul to have been correct about the rapture in 1 Thessalonians 4 and 1 Corinthians 15? And what about the promises in Isaiah 2, 11, etc.? That kind of thinking tends to leave a person void of hope, peace and joy, and frankly, I see no blessing at all in a life lived with that being part of a Christian's belief system.

That is why it is so important to understand the message of Daniel two. So, we might ask, exactly what should we remember about this message?

The first thing about the message is it belongs to you and me as Gentiles. Daniel 2:4 to 7:28 was written in Aramaic (not Arabic!). Aramaic was the language of the Gentile world in those days. The entire book is important, but this emphasizes the importance of those six chapters to non-Jews. It must be understood that all four kingdoms in the vision are Gentile, and that Israel eventually came under the control of all four: the Babylonians, the Medes and Persians, the Greeks and the Romans.

And, since 605 BC when Daniel was taken captive, the land of Israel has not been under a genuine Davidic Jewish monarchy. The fact of the matter is God was showing to Nebuchadnezzar, and to us, that this ongoing anti-Semitic Gentile world will one day be destroyed to be replaced by the reign of David's greatest Son, Jesus the Christ. In fact, the dream was in answer to the king's prayer (2:29) regarding just such a matter.

Second, the message firmly emphasizes that God alone is Master of both time and world events. Nothing in the realm of Jewish and Gentile world politics happens by random accident. Though God does not orchestrate death and tragedy, yet He most certainly corrals humanity's evil and uses it to bring about the fruition of His plan (2:21). And that includes who becomes a prime minister, president or monarch.

Third, the message declares in no uncertain terms that the world's greatest Jew will become the world's greatest King. Have another look at Zechariah 14 and Revelation 19. During the millennium Jesus will rule with a rod of iron and will summarily smash into subjection anyone, commoner or aristocrat, who might resist His sovereignty during His reign. His kingdom will fill the entire earth, and the saved of the ages will reign with Him. There will be no place on this planet where anyone might live separate from the powerful and authoritative theocratic reign of the King of kings and Lord of lords. Satan will be bound and peace will abound. Such peace, prosperity, restoration and blessing will never happen during the Times of the Gentiles, no matter who leads and no matter what they do. Bank on that.

Funny, but it seems this is the part of the message most Christians just cannot accept. A careful study might reveal they do not understand "redemption". To redeem something is to buy it back; to own it by act of creation and then to own it by paying a price for it after it had been taken away. That principle applies to humanity and to the earth. Isaiah and other Hebrew prophets spoke of such aspects of creation's redemption, but those texts are most often rejected out of hand by multitudes who claim the title of Christian. Jesus died for the sins of humanity, and though the earth did not sin against God, it has been subjected to the curse of man's sin since the Garden. The ancient Hebrew prophets spoke clearly of the time when the curse will be lifted (e.g. Isaiah 2,11,65, Ezekiel 47, Joel 3, etc.), and that time is coming. Just as sure as the sun will rise tomorrow morning, that time is coming.

We see from this that death and hell get nothing from God.

Saved humans will have their spirits, souls and immortal glorified bodies for all eternity. Further, the earth will be "restored" (God's precise word, not mine) for 1000 years, and just prior to the eternal state it will be burned by an inconceivable fire (2 Peter 3:10) which will destroy every evidence of human rebellion and deprivation. There will not be even one cursed molecule left over from the old earth. Lucifer and his minions will only get hell, and not even one square inch of this planet. Though Satan is currently the "god of this world" (2 Corinthians 4:4), that will all change soon. Millions in the last few months have been talking about "change we can believe in". Well, change is coming indeed, but it won't be the kind they have in mind!

Fourth, the message is clear about Jesus' kingdom being on this earth. The four great empires were all on this earth as secular history bears out. The stone cut out without hands will destroy every vestige of them and will grow in their place. In fact, Daniel says very clearly it will fill the entire earth, not heaven. See again Isaiah 2:1-4 for a snapshot as to how all this will look.

And, what should this message do for us? It should make us aware of the fact that the taking out of the church is imminent. That should always be our prevailing thought. But, there is more.

We can rest at peace. If there is one commodity about which the world knows nothing it is peace. Of course, since we are presently living on this cursed planet we have natural concerns about any number of matters that affect our livelihoods and families. Yet, we do not fear as the world fears. We do not fear Ahmadinejad because he is a pawn in God's hand. We do not fear Kim Jong Il for he, too, is an impotent despot on a leash. We do not fear a falling stock market and a devalued dollar for our citizenship is not of this world. We do not fear that some sleazy politicians in Washington wish to remove our liberty for we understand real liberty is at hand.

And, if the Lord's coming is further delayed we see how Christians can face death without fear. Though death is the enemy of all mankind, yet even now we can speak directly to the Grim Reaper instead of talking about him (1 Corinthians 15:55). No fame, no amount of money and no credentials awarded by any human institution can offer that!

Further, we can see the future — a blessing given to all who are believers if they would simply accept it. We are not stunned by any turn of world events, for we know what is in store. In fact, about the only thing that surprises us is that Jesus has not come for His church before now! Perhaps the only question we might ask in closing takes us back to the beginning. If Nebuchadnezzar the pagan king could characterize this terminal generation that has so much more knowledge and information than he had, how do you think he might describe it in light of its vile and sordid unbelief? DLM

Chapter 30

4 November 2008—What Happened?

~ ~ ~ ~ ~

On Wednesday morning after the presidential election I received a call from someone who asked about the fall-out from the Obama win and what it might mean for our country. At noon the same day two more people asked the same question and what measures they might take to prepare for the hard-times they are certain will come. From those questions and countless others being asked on talk radio, at church assemblies, at coffee klatches, etc., we can assume a significant segment of our population is now concerned about the Obama presidency. At least some are nothing less than fearful. Are such fears justified from a biblical perspective? Have we been warned about these matters? Let's take a look.

This article must be prefaced with a statement of non-partisanship. I am strongly conservative and I live and vote that way, but the issues facing our republic and we Christians who live here go beyond mere political parties. What divides our government is a political aisle in Washington, but the real arena of division is in the heart of America. That is, what divides our people is the ever-escalating battle over that which is right and that which is wrong. Period.

For almost two hundred years the words and original intent of our Founding Fathers were not questioned by our country's citizenry. We long acknowledged the influence Jesus Christ and the Bible had on those cardinal principles established and embraced in our founding documents. Islam, Hinduism, Buddhism and other such pagan religions held no sway in the hearts of our Founders. Socialism was anathema. It seems very clear, however, that has all changed.

Speaking of change

Change that we have all heard so much about is indeed coming. The important question, though, has to do with the kind of change. During the campaign nobody told us exactly what distinctions to expect, while many had a pretty good idea they might not be good. Though there were some very major differences between individual candidates at all levels, the fact is if we dig deeper we find that which is being touted as "change" is not something totally different from what we've been seeing for the last several decades. It just has more of a blue tinge than red now. Beginning with the Scopes Trial and the Humanist Manifesto I in the 1920s and 30s, and continuing until today it is very easy to see an overall cultural and political shift toward anti-God humanism. The only change Obama will bring is a quantum leap in that direction.

Consider the last few years. Mr. William Jefferson Clinton ignored Islamic threats while concurrently bringing shame upon himself, his family, the country and the presidency all evidently without remorse. Mr. George Walker Bush, while as a sitting American president, declared Islam to be "one of the world's great religions" and officially celebrated Ramadan in the White House. Keith Ellison, a newly-elected congressman recently swore allegiance to America with his hand on a Koran, an action that many believe to be a type of oxymoron.

Mr. Barack Hussein Obama, it is believed, will simply accelerate the degradation. How? To the best of his ability he will make his virulently anti-God opinions national law. He be-

174 4 November 2008—What Happened?

lieves it is perfectly fine to murder babies who somehow survive abortions. He, along with former president Jimmy Carter, is ecstatic about jumping head-long into the Middle East "peace process" whereby Israel will be forced to give more of her land to her (and our) enemies. It appears he has absolutely no nationalistic loyalties and no tolerance for those who do have them. He endorses the perverted homosexual agenda with no hesitation. And to each of these, and other anti-American special-interest groups, he owes some major favors for their political support. And, we cannot forget he is a flaming socialist who disagrees with capitalism, the right to keep and bear arms and other aspects of traditional American liberties. The recent election, it seems to many, simply moved the anti-God, anti-Bible, anti-nationalist, anti-capitalism, anti-liberty agenda from a somewhat subdued level to a wild-eyed, in-your-face extravaganza with all stops pulled out and discarded.

So, what really happened?

For quite a while a very vocal part of America's electorate has been demanding God take His hand off our national affairs. Well, it is quite possible He, perhaps running out of patience, did just that on 4 November 2008. Understand though, that is certainly not to say God is a Republican. Said another way, we are not to be interested in whose side God is on in politics, but who among us is on His side. The election indicated most aren't. We just can't seem to accept the fact that it is not Washington, but God who leads, establishes moral law, defines righteousness and dictates conduct and lifestyles. The bottom line is we follow or He punishes and, if repentance is not forthcoming He ultimately judges. It seems nationally we have gotten what we have demanded, and now we must accept the consequences.

We should all detest Obama's preacher, the racist hate-monger Jeremiah Wright, but like the wicked Caiaphas who did not understand the implication of his words (John 11:49-53), so also did the evil Wright not understand the implication of his words when he said America's chickens have come home to roost.

Maybe they have. Maybe our national inclination toward a secular society and a godless government has brought its consequences. And maybe the word "uncomfortable" will fall tragically short of describing the reality of it all. I find it interesting how God sometimes uses the words of the wicked to point to something of far greater importance than that of their original intent.

Who suffers in hard times?

Well, what about Christians who live and vote as faithfully and biblically as possible? Will they suffer with the reprobates should hard times come as a result of God removing His hand? Yes. Some say that is not fair. Folks, this whole thing is not about fairness! It is about God's people being called from, yet having to live in, a sin-sick, evil world where most all major choices and consequences touch the lives of most all people, good and bad. Righteous Daniel suffered with rebellious Judah though he was personally innocent. History is replete with such examples. The greater portion of the Lord's people on this planet is suffering this very moment. They are not more deserving of hardship than we; they are simply living under circumstances where deprivation and evil abound.

We can stand on the fact Christians will not go through any portion of the seven year tribulation, but that is not to say Christians will not see tribulation of any kind if the Lord's return is longer delayed. It is true Paul told the Thessalonians the church will escape the wrath that is to come upon the world (1 Thessalonians 1:10), but it is also true many Christians died martyr's deaths in those very same days, and many are even doing so today in communist and Islamic countries.

We, however, do not despair. We believe God is still sovereign, that He is able to take care of us by seeing us through whatever happens as a result of our growing national rebellion and probably soon-coming judgment. And, even more encouraging is the fact Jesus' return is imminent. That singular event is *the* Blessed Hope for the godly (Titus 2:11).

So, what might be God's punishment and judgment upon a God -hating culture? It could be the loss of our affluent lifestyle followed by the loss of our liberties, and in that order. One hundred years ago Americans valued liberty over wealth by understanding being free is more important than being slaves under government management. On Election Day we saw clearly how that has been turned around. It appears that many who voted chose to give up liberty for government supervision of their lives especially in the areas of housing and health care, both of which are abysmally sub-standard when administered by the government. Instead of the traditional American view of manhood being that of self-reliance, independence and freedom from government intervention, many opted for government sponsored cradle-to-grave provision thus selling their God-given, blood-bought birthright for a bowl of beans (Genesis 25:29-34).

It may be that God is about to smash our national god — money. It is possible He will allow continuing financial difficulties in order that we understand the futility of godless materialism. There is no inherent evil in possessions; the sin is in our making them gods to which everything else becomes subservient. Secularism has brought us to the place of rank idolatry. Like Judah which was temporarily displaced, or maybe even like Israel which was scattered, God might be in the process of giving us exactly what we have wanted — a God-free society. The piper, however, must be paid for the dance.

Is all of this inevitable?

Can this secular juggernaut with all its godlessness and destruction be stopped? No. The clear indications we see in prophecy, though not pleasant, are also not hard to understand. If a person will step back from the unfolded time-line of all history (past, present and future) it is easy to see how humanity has always demanded God get out of the way and that the race will continue to make this same demand all the way to the end. From the spiritual fall of mankind until the Great White Throne Judgment the growing division between creature and Creator is easily seen. *It will not change because the inherent evil of the unregenerate human heart does not change.* And one of the contributing factors to the dramatic increase in the speed and size of the division is the fact you won't hear the previous statement from the overwhelming majority of pulpits on Sunday mornings. It, you see, is too offensive to modern man's refined sensibilities.

Well, what about a reprieve?

If it cannot be stopped, can we get a reprieve? Maybe. No man knows the details of God's plan so a definitive answer is not possible. It could be that our world and our country are far beyond the point-of-no-return. Yet, God is not only sovereign but also attentive to the fasting and prayers of His people when His name and glory are our genuine motives. If, however, our request for a reprieve is selfish in nature I do not expect relief. This principle is clearly explained in James 4:1-4.

Preparation

If hard times are coming is there something we can do to prepare? I think so. First and foremost is we must stay on our knees before God with the prayer of Daniel 9:4. Next, get out of debt as quickly as possible. Drive the same cars and wear the same clothes longer. Do not be influenced by the simple-minded who use credit cards which are not zeroed monthly to eat out often, buy toys, take trips and make other foolish and unaffordable purchases. They play the one-up game with their friends with most every purchase be it a house, vehicle, or whatever. We must teach our children to be independent and self-sufficient; to see wealth as a tool instead of a god; to make choices and purchases based upon biblical principles and to understand we are ambassadors in this world and not residents.

Conclusion

There are some other things we would do well to keep in mind. The world hated Jesus because He called it evil. When you bring this same indictment against the world expect those who subscribe to, or who see no sin in toleration of abortion, homosexual "marriages", illegitimacy, government intervention, gross debt, socialism, etc., to hate you, also. Remember the book of Daniel gives us insight into how demonic hosts work tirelessly in the satanic effort of influencing entire nations and their leadership. To think the same is not happening presently is to ignore the obvious.

Look for any number of abominable practices to become part and parcel of national policy, but the three big ones will probably be abortion/infanticide, homosexual "marriages" and anti-Semitism. The assimilation of monstrous ideologies and conduct into mainstream society usually happens in stages. As was the case with abortion and homosexuality so will be anti-Semitism as it moves from abhorrence to acceptance. It does not have very far to go.

The pro-God and thus the pro-Bible, pro-life and pro-family way of thinking, living and raising children will be viewed as abnormal and considered undesirable. Government schools will be the key tool in destroying any biblical foundation a child might have, and in restructuring that child's thinking. Just like Germany in 1933. We would be wise to remember the words of Baldur von Schirach, the Hitler Youth Leader: "...Whoever marches in the Hitler Youth is not a number among millions but the soldier of an idea. The individual member's value to the whole is determined by the degree to which he is permeated by the idea. The best Hitler Youth, irrespective of rank and office, is he who completely surrenders himself to the National Socialist world view." After reading Obama's national public education plan it seems he wants parents out and the government in regarding the education of our children. In a nutshell the fallout from this election will be a very serious escalation in the battle for the hearts and minds of our children.

In the analysis God will use the results of the election to bring about His plan. Believe it! Then one day soon we will view the events of this world while laughing with our Lord about man's utter impotence and foolishness (Psalm 2). Every godless president, king, prime minister, etc., will grovel before Jesus Christ in a sort of primeval fear, knowing their horrifying end has come. They boasted, cursed God, ignored the Bible and otherwise blasphemed His name. At that appointed time they will give account...and we will witness it all. So, take heart in all that comes. Read the last chapter and see God wins.

Finally, we are commanded to pray for our civil authorities (1 Timothy 2). What will be the result? Only God knows, but our responsibility is to pray. And while on our knees we might ask God to give us powerful faculties to use in making future political choices. There is absolutely no excuse for God's people not to have seen this assault upon His divine order coming. DLM

Chapter 31

Inevitable Global Conflict

~ ~ ~ ~ ~

We have all seen it before. The scene: the final five of an international beauty contest have their last chance to impress the judges. While the others are sequestered each contestant is asked in turn what would be the primary goal of her reign should she win the crown. You have a sneaking suspicion you already know the answer and, sure enough, the young woman says, "I will do all I can to work toward world peace." The host smiles broadly as the audience responds with heavy applause and shrill whistles. The only thing that overshadows the absurdity of the answer is its predictability.

What makes all this sadly humorous is not the sincerity of the young candidate. It is not even that her words about world peace fall flat for lack of credibility, because ignorance and naivety are to be expected in youth. The obvious, but unspoken truth is the fact that world peace is not going to happen no matter what she, or anyone else does. Maybe even she suspects that is the truth of the matter. The host knows it is, the sponsors know it is, the owners of the pageant know it is and certainly at least most in the audience also know it is. But, with the world in turmoil such uninformed answers sound good and assuages fear in the hearts of some, even if they know it is all a crock of politically-correct hogwash.

Two things need to be faced head-on. First is the fact that world peace is not going to happen in this dispensation. Period. Second is the fact that nobody wants to admit it, at least nobody whoever wants to be considered as a person with political or social credentials. Feel-good-about-the-world protocol demands that people must address alternatives to coming global warfare and to summarily dismiss discussions of its inevitability as the unsophisticated ravings of religious lunatics living out there on the fringe of society.

What is this illusive commodity so many are talking about? Trying to define peace is like trying to define love. We all have some idea about it, but specific agreement is impossible to reach. Forget lexicographers and their long-winded definitions. In general conversation among normal people peace is often defined as "absence of conflict". It can have physical and emotional applications, etc., but you get the general idea. Further, "peace" cannot be equated with "freedom", for a castaway on a small deserted island might not be at risk for robbery or assault, but he is not really free.

The truth is that no human has ever been able to construct a political system that guarantees freedom from any and all threats of bodily harm, loss of property, government expropriation of private property, murder, assault, etc. Further, no humanly constructed political system can guarantee your country will not be attacked by belligerent neighbors, or by some despot on the other side of the world who might use the money you spend on gasoline to buy a single missile with a single warhead with your name on it.

It is amazing that so many allegedly smart people cannot understand that just because they personally mean no harm to anyone else, their enemy does not live according to that same standard. I am reminded of a totally absurd comment the foolish former British Prime Minister Neville Chamberlain said late in his life about WW II. He said everything would have been alright, "If only Hitler hadn't lied." Don't laugh — there are many Cham-

berlains in leadership positions in our country this very moment
and some of them want you to elect them president.

Well, what about religion? Surely, peace can be found in religion, can't it? Tell that to the multitudes killed by the Moslem
hordes in their crusades to subjugate the world to Islam (both
early and modern), and also to those other multitudes killed in
the Roman Catholic crusades in their efforts to subjugate the
Middle East to the popes. The fact of the matter is no man-
made religion, from a tribal level to one international in scope,
has ever brought genuine peace to humanity, and none ever
will. If that is true there must be a reason. And there is, indeed,
a reason.

The operative word is "man-made", for therein lies the problem.
Humanly inspired religions begin in the hearts of men and
women who believe they have a better idea about whom or
what to worship as "god" and how to live in harmony with each
other. It is a very bad start because the human heart, the seat of
thought, will and emotion is terribly wicked, and hence anything springing from it is naturally tainted. Though we do not
like to admit it that is the truth. God said, "The heart is more
deceitful than all else and is desperately sick; Who can understand it?" (Jeremiah 17:9).

Well, what about a consortium of efforts? Suppose a political
entity like the UN would join forces with a church of some
kind? Wouldn't that work? Such an effort is in the hopper this
very moment, but no, it will not work, either. It will have its
result, but it will not be global peace.

In 1993 Bishop William Swing of the California Diocese of the
Episcopal Church was asked to formulate some sort of interfaith
service to help mark the 50th anniversary of the UN. Not only
did he come up with an interfaith service, but an interfaith religion to promote tolerance among all people of faith around the
world; a religion that would become the spiritual side of the
United Nations. It is called the United Religions Initiative

(URI) and it became an official non-governmental organization (NGO) connected with the UN in 2001.

Much could be said about this religious monster, but it is sufficient presently only to say it could very well become an important part of the coming harlot church of the tribulation. In fact, its global assembly this year will be 30 November through 5 December in Mayapur, West Bengal, India with a theme of *Pilgrims of Peace — Many Paths, One Purpose* (very ecumenical sounding!). The URI will also be involved in the UN International Day of Peace in September. The bottom line, though, is that the political UN and its religious consort, the URI, will never eradicate war and discord from the face of the earth. Both entities are corrupt and rotten to their cores because both are absolutely void of fundamental Christian doctrine and the biblical worldview. Further, they are saturated with global feel-good-tolerance for every form of paganism you might imagine. All of which, by the way, will soon feel the blast of God's righteous indignation and wrath.

If, then, it is impossible for humanity to prevent global conflict, what is being done about the situation? The first thing the world is doing is ignoring God in the matter. God has said quite clearly this planet is going to come under a world ruler whose ruthlessness is unprecedented. God calls him the anti-Christ, the son of perdition, etc. He will be energized by Satan and will kill anyone who gets in his way. During the very first part of the seven-year period in which he will operate untold multitudes will die because of war, famine, disease and wild animals (Revelation 6:1-8). God has said the only way of escaping this world-wide catastrophe is through faith in Jesus Christ, and His coming for His church in what is commonly called the rapture.

Now, since all that is ignored by the majority of human beings, what is humanity doing to deal with what some readily admit is the inevitable? Some are wringing their hands, in deep distress about their powerlessness over their own lives and futures.

Some are supporting political candidates who are saying they have the solution, and it has to do with change, redistribution of the earth's wealth, political and religious toleration, loving everybody, etc. Others are moving to remote areas where they believe they will be able to live off the land and defend themselves when total lawlessness becomes the norm. Still others are trusting in science and technology to ward off universal catastrophe. A good example of this is the "doomsday" seed vault in Svalbard, Norway built to protect food crop seed from war, climate changes, etc.

The vault opened on 26 February 2008 and is called, "...our insurance policy" by Norway's Prime Minister Jens Stoltenberg. He also referred to it as "Noah's Ark". The European Commission President, Jose Manuel Barroso called it "...a frozen Garden of Eden." (foxnews.com story 26 Feb 08, Norway Formally Opens Arctic Doomsday Seed Vault). At .4°F they expect the seeds to last 1000 years.

In a way, all this global/social fear has been a financial boon for some. News companies are cashing in on humanity's fearful and somewhat morbid interest in the demise of the race by publishing stories similar to those usually found in smut-sheets, the super market tabloids. On the same day, and on the same web site as the seed story was another headline, "Scientist Predict When World Will End" (foxnews.com 26 Feb 08). Now, who would not click on that one?!

Scientists now say life has been around on earth for 3.7 billion years (during the first 3 billion we were pond scum), that the earth will be pulled into the sun in 7.6 billion years and vaporized, but that life on earth will end long before then. However, another brilliant scientist says the answer is in "taming" an asteroid to do a low pass over the earth every couple thousand years or so in order to nudge the planet into a higher orbit in order to escape the sun's pull. Can you believe the idiocy of some of those people? Yet, it is those same people who are saying we Christians are the ones who are nuts for believing in

God!!

The bottom line is actually quite simple. Social unrest and worldwide political turmoil will continue to escalate. Jesus will return for His church (an imminent event!) and remove her to heaven before He pours out His blistering wrath on a world that seethes in its hatred of Him and His people. Things will become so bad people will actually desire death, but will be unable to kill themselves. At the end of that seven year period known as "the tribulation" the world will literally and totally be in a state of dismal ruin as a result of humanity's bitter rebellion against God. Along with the righteous wrath of God being evident during this time will probably be man's use of every known weapon of destruction in the world. Add to that the impact of the natural result of world war — gut-wrenching famine and the spread of every disease pathogen imaginable. URI or no URI.

At the end of that seven years Jesus will return to this earth, specifically to the Mt. of Olives just across the Kidron Valley from Jerusalem, and will inaugurate 1000 years of Theocracy. The saved of the ages will reign with Him as His coheirs, and all human rebellion will be smashed like a clay jar is smashed with a heavy piece of re-bar. Finally, there will be peace on earth...and not before then. Yes, it is all in the Bible...the only book with 100% accuracy 100% of the time.

So, what should we do? Exactly what God has been saying for millennia. Be ready for the next event on the calendar — the rapture of the church. It is my deepest conviction that in these closing days of this dispensation God is raising up a caste of men whose major responsibility is to declare these things, to warn people of "the wrath to come" (1 Thessalonians 1:10) and to do so even at the risk of being labeled reactionary.

Peace...? The UN...? The URI...? The ecumenical movement...? A seed vault...??!! Don't be foolish. DLM

Chapter 32

Giving Away Israel

~ ~ ~ ~ ~

Several years ago media pictures from Israel showed Israeli police officers at barricades prohibiting the entrance of non-resident Jews into Gaza as they prepared to remove the resident Jews. Ariel Sharon, the man who in the beginning begged Jews to settle the Gaza area, is the same man presently responsible for forcibly removing them from Gaza. Sharon is desperate in his desire for the world to see Israel as taking the moral high ground in the war against Moslem attempts to destroy his country, and he believes giving away more Jewish land to their sworn enemies will help do that. He also believes that "consolidating Israel" will put their country into a better defensive position. He is wrong.

Never has the giving away of Jewish land to Arabs resulted in either. No matter how much of her own land Israel gives to her enemies and no matter how much Jewish blood soaks into the sand of their country, the world will never recognize Israel as taking the moral high ground in any matter, and especially in her struggle against the Arabs. Furthermore, never has such action resulted in the Arabs dropping their often repeated goal of the total annihilation of Israel.

One of the characteristics of the Jewish people is their longing to be accepted by the world community. Their desire to "be like the other nations" is actually historic (1 Samuel 8). The truth of the matter, however, is it will not happen. Nothing they do will ever cause the world to view them as regular, normal or acceptable. The world readily accepts Cuba, North Korea, Sudan, Syria, China and other brutal nations whose national flags are soaked in the blood of tens of millions, but Israel simply does not qualify. In fact, Israel is not even allowed to fully participate in the activities of the UN — the only nation so treated. Why is this so? The simplified answer is they are Jews. There are numerous details associated with that answer, but in short that is it. They are Jews. And the world hates the Jews.

On August 19th former U.S. Ambassador to Morocco, Marc Ginsberg, told Fox News viewers that the "disengagement" was a good thing, and that it will help insure Israel's security. Mr. Ginsberg is a highly respected diplomat who is often sought after by news organizations for his commentary on the Middle East. He was raised in that part of the world, speaks several languages of that area and has academic and diplomatic credentials which are impeccable. So, how could a man of such caliber be so mistaken regarding this matter?

The major reason is Mr. Ginsberg views the situation from a secular perspective; that is, he has no interest in what God has to say about the matter, and he does not consider the complete history of Israel and the land as being of any importance. This attitude is not held by Ginsberg alone. Secretary of State Condoleezza Rice and even President George Bush hold the same view point. In essence, the fact that the land belongs to God and that He gave it to the descendants of Abraham through his only legitimate son Isaac in an unconditional covenant has no bearing at all in their minds. What a mistake!

Some believe that since President Bush and Secretary Rice have some degree of "religion" they should know better. Not necessarily. Rice's father was a preacher, but that does not automatically insure she understands God's covenants with Israel. And, does not mean she pays any attention to them. Obviously she does not. Mr. Bush's religious background is rooted in denominations whose leadership and membership historically ignore the covenants. He might be a man of prayer and perhaps he might be many other things religiously speaking, but when it comes to God's foreign policy statement regarding His people Israel and their land Mr. Bush is either ignorant, or he has chosen to disregard that which he knows to be the truth in an effort to capitalize on political expediency.

If the problem is one of ignorance he is without excuse, for the truth can be easily discovered and just as easily understood. Further, if he knows these things, but ignores them for whatever political reasons then he is lining himself and our country up for the direct judgment of God. You see, folks, though God is indeed patient and full of grace, He is also a God who has an end to His patience and he will not stand still very long while some human being thumbs his nose at Him.

Well, what about the Arabs? Are the Arabs grateful for the pullout? No. They say there is nothing to be grateful to Israel for because it is their land anyway. This infamous lie is believed and perpetuated by untold numbers of people who are either ignorant or anti-Semitic or both. Even Condoleezza Rice sounded like an Arab when she said that as sorry as she feels for the expelled Jews and all the heartache and problems it has caused, Israel must not think this is all the giving they will have to do — Gaza is only the first step.

The fact of the matter is that giving away Jewish land will not appease the Arabs. How do we know this? Easy — they are saying so! On August 19th Mahmoud Abbas, the current head of the Palestinian Authority said while in Gaza City, "Today we are celebrating the liberation of Gaza and the northern West Bank; tomorrow we will celebrate the liberation of Jerusalem." Hamas and Islamic Jihad (Moslem terrorist groups who will, according to the U.S. State Department, give up terrorism for civil responsibilities such as repairing potholes once they are part of the Palestinian government...some very simple people actually believe this) have stated strongly and without equivocation that they will continue to kill Jews even after the disengagement from Gaza is complete. Visit some Arab websites, read their commentary and see how many times you see the nation of Israel on their maps.

What more will it take for our own government and that of Mr. Ariel Sharon to face the truth? Mahmoud Abbas takes tens of millions of American tax dollars every year and quickly grabs up any land the Sharon administration hands him. But, not once is he genuinely obligated to do anything in return. And the reason is he does not want peace. The Arabs want every Jew driven into the sea, they want every square inch of Israel as their own and they want Jerusalem as their capital. We know this because they have said so. The problem is Mr. Bush, Mr. Sharon and others say, "Naw. They don't really mean what they are saying." This reminds me so much of Neville Chamberlain and his foolish and naïve "peace in our time" speech – just before England was plunged into WW2.

Some actually believe that retreating to Israel "proper" will make Israel safer for two reasons. First, Abbas will be so appreciative to Israel for giving up Gaza that he will rein in the Moslem terrorists. Second, Israel will be in a better defensive position and will no longer have to use troops to watch Gaza for terrorist and weapons infiltration. The first is not happening and will never happen. The second is the Arabs themselves have already admitted they will use Gaza as a platform from which to launch attacks against Israel "proper".

Sharon says he reserves the right to counterattack if necessary. Oh, yeah? What do you suppose the world reaction would be should the IDF launce defensive incursion operations into the future sovereign state of Palestine? It would be Desert Storm all over again, but this time the objective would be Israel and not Iraq.

This is a very sad time in the history of America and modern Israel. God is being ignored by both countries regarding these matters. Faith would demand that our president stand on the truth of God's word without regard to human political expediency just like Joshua did when he conquered that same land over 3400 years ago. Some of Joshua's decisions did not make sense humanly speaking, but God honored his obedience by driving out the pagan inhabitants and giving the land to His people.

Mr. Sharon is not a religious Jew and therefore could not care less about what God did for Moses, Joshua and others among his ancestors. Sadly, his people will pay a great price. Two-thirds will die before they acknowledge Jesus as their Messiah. And America will eventually be among those camped against Israel. We are in the shadow of those events today. DLM

Chapter 33

The Source of Truth

~ ~ ~ ~ ~

Nobody would argue that things are changing all around us. Take a look at how some things were about 100 years ago.

♦ The average life expectancy was 47 years.
♦ Only 8% of homes had telephones.
♦ There were only 8000 automobiles and only 144 miles of paved roads.
♦ The average wage was 22 cents per hour.
♦ 90% of all physicians had no college education.
♦ The population of Las Vegas was 30.
♦ Sugar was 4 cents per pound.
♦ Most women washed their hair only once a month, and used egg yolks for shampoo.

We can look at this list and laugh, because we find life 100 years ago somewhat primitive. But, one of the big differences today is modern humanity's almost insatiable demand for information. We believe it is critical to be informed about anything and everything and we want that information available immediately no matter where we might be.

Many people would not leave home in the mornings without watching a weather report, listening to the local radio station's obituary notice and the international news. We want to know how commodities are trading, what the stock markets in Asia and Europe are doing, what is happening in Washington, D.C. and who died last night. We check our several email accounts numerous times each day to see who is sending what information. And, it is all done from our computers (home and office), and from our touch-screen telephones that can tell us the location and directions to the closest coffee shop.

The problem with our fast-paced world is not that we can get consumer information from almost any location at blazing speed, for the impact of such information is mostly limited to the ease at which we live our daily lives. The problem we are facing in this modern information age has to do with the source of information we use to shape our world view. And, that is where things become critical.

A person's worldview is the standard by which they interpret life. Their worldview establishes their priorities and becomes their template for measuring truth, morality, integrity, etc. And, the crux of the matter is a person's worldview is formed by what they have chosen to be their source of truth. That is not a bad thing if they have chosen the eternal and immutable word of God, but to choose any other source is an error with unimaginably terrible eternal consequences.

Christians are not worried about the future because we understand the next event on God's calendar is the rapture of the church, and that event is imminent. Though we are indeed concerned about the current political landscape, both national and international, and though we desire a morally stable society and a world where totalitarianism is no more, yet we also understand such things will not happen as long as humanity rules the planet. We believe strongly in the stewardship of natural resources and we decry waste and pollution.

However, we also understand this world is not our home, and that we are simply ambassadors to a world system that is totally in rebellion against our King for whose pleasure we serve. But, we have read the Book; we know the truth about the present and the future; we know what is happening and why, and we know what is next and what follows that. Said succinctly, we see what is happening and believe we are soon to be out of here. Said another way, we are soon to be recalled by the King.

On the other hand, the vast majority of people could not care less regarding what God has said about current events. They see "religion" as a sort of mythological panacea to which only the ignorant and unsophisticated subscribe. They are void of faith, and are deceived into believing humanity is solely at the mercy of natural forces that cannot be fully controlled by the mind and efforts of mankind. They believe they can make the world better by redistributing wealth, educating everyone, increasing taxes, blindly tolerating every religion and culture, cleaning up the planet and reducing everybody's carbon footprint. At the same time, they also believe the world could be reduced to rubble by the impact of a large asteroid, exploding super volcanoes, powerful earthquakes and associated tidal waves, and other natural phenomena that might increase or decrease the earth's ambient temperature. In short, they live to a great degree in fear.

Further, they give undo credence to things like the following description of an asteroid impact with earth.

> *By the time you get up to a mile-wide asteroid, you are working in the 1 million megaton range. This asteroid has the energy that's 10 million times greater than the bomb that fell on Hiroshima. It's able to flatten everything for 100 to 200 miles out from ground zero. In other words, if a mile-wide asteroid were to directly hit New York City, the force of the impact probably would completely flatten every single thing from Washington D.C. to Boston, and would cause extensive damage perhaps 1,000 miles out -- that's as far away as Chicago. The amount of dust and debris thrown up into the at-*

mosphere would block out the sun and cause most living things on the planet to perish. If an asteroid that big were to land in the ocean, it would cause massive tidal waves hundreds of feet high that would completely scrub the coastlines in the vicinity.

In other words, if an asteroid strikes Earth, it will be a really, really bad day no matter how big it is. If the asteroid is a mile in diameter, it's likely to wipe out life on the planet. Let's hope that doesn't happen anytime soon! (http://science.howstuffworks.com/asteroid-hits-earth.htm cited 17March10)

Many people go to such sources as Discovery Channel and History Channel to get their information about the future of the planet. There is some good to be found in those resources. However, when it comes to issues addressed by the Bible they fall far short of the truth. And, by the way, the Bible does address the destruction of the earth. It will indeed be destroyed, but not until God is ready and it will happen by His method (2 Peter 3:9-13). The destruction of earth, however, will have no effect upon Christians for we will be alive and well living in the eternal state associated with the new heavens and the new earth. Because God has clearly laid out His plan we do not fear planetary destruction.

Everybody views and interprets events in one of two different ways — biblical or secular. Christians examine everything through the lens of scripture, and because of this, we are at peace being fully aware of where we are on the time-line of history. Unbelievers, however, know absolutely nothing about the scriptural viewpoint and are left to interpret everything from a defective, secular viewpoint.

The fact is we are living in the post-modern era and people now understand that science and technology cannot answer all questions, cure all diseases and prevent all disasters. These people are not imbeciles and can clearly see that terrible events are on the near horizon. Yet, they have no peace about things because the system they use to interpret world events offers none. Doom and gloom are coming and they know it.

There is, however, another aspect of these mega destructive forces that must be noted. During the tribulation period, when Christians will be in heaven, the earth will indeed experience cataclysmic destruction from various sources. John noted some of them as he recorded the book of Revelation. The strongest earthquake in world history will happen during that time when God pours out His wrath on an earth that has completely rejected Him (Revelation 16:17ff.). This earthquake will be unprecedented in power and will have unimaginable geological impact upon both mountain and island ranges around the globe. No place on the planet will be left untouched.

Calamitous events will impact food production. At one point (Revelation 8:7) a third of the earth, a third of all the trees, and all green grass will be burned up. This will impact air quality along with food production. The sea will no longer be a dependable food source and a third of marine commerce will be destroyed (Revelation 8:8,9).

Secular TV programming seen each evening indicates people believe something dreadful is on the near horizon. Broadcast producers would not dedicate so much time and money to this theme if they did not believe it. The recent rash of earthquakes in Haiti, Chile, Taiwan, Sumatra and the continued warnings that the San Andreas "big one" in California is overdue indicate something catastrophic is expected. Add to that the convincing evidence that a disastrous global financial collapse seems very certain, that high unemployment will continue and that the value of the dollar will trend downward. Further, the fact that China owns right at $1 trillion of U.S. debt is enough to promote insomnia, and a government that believes it can spend its way out of debt and onward to prosperity is nothing less than economic idiocy.

If that is not enough to worry about, think about the strong possibility of other Islamic attacks on the U.S. mainland that might target financial centers, power grids and the petro-chemical industries, all of which will immediately be felt at food stores and gas stations. As we have seen, this could result in the imposition of martial law and the suspension of civil liberty, all with very dire consequences.

So, when you boil it all down, the important questions are where does a person go for information about what is happening, and what does a person believe as a result. If you get your information from the secular world you probably believe mankind is destined to continue plodding along until something comes along humanity can't handle, and it all goes in the toilet...it is over. What a terrible, pessimistic, godless way to live!

If, however, you believe that God is still sovereign, and if you believe what He has said regarding life in the end-times, you are on the right track. It is true that the world, and even our country, could see difficult times if the return of Jesus for His church is delayed much longer, but that is not reason for despair. Such events should cause us to look up and to be watchful, for our redemption is getting close. And, for those Christians with the means to grow food and access fresh water, those days might be a means of helping those who cannot help themselves.

Remember, the important thing is to believe what God has said about these things. The biblical belief system and worldview brings peace and certainty when the world is falling down around us. The secular worldview that most people depend upon can't do this because it is totally corrupt and flawed. Thus the godless not only die, but die in fear. DLM

Chapter 34

Why the World Can't Bury Titanic

~ ~ ~ ~ ~

In 1997 James Cameron wrote, directed and co-produced "Titanic", one of the most dramatic movies of all time. The movie broke established records of that time with a production budget of $200 million and box-office receipts of $1.8 billion. Not bad for a man who dreamed up the project because he was simply interested in shipwrecks.

Much has been written about the disaster, and many thoughtful essays have been published comparing the modern world's deplorable situation with that of the stricken "Titanic". With April 15, 2012 being the 100th anniversary of that terrible night, special interest in the tragedy has been generated. But, actually little information of real significance has been revealed since 1997. Since Robert Ballard discovered the wreck in 1985 everybody has come to know the story and most of the details, yet the subject never becomes ho-hum.

So, why does a dissolving hulk in 12,000 feet of seawater still command such interest? Is it because the unexpected, mind-numbing loss is conversely equal to Titanic's unprecedented supremacy and luxury? Is it simply rooted in humanity's naturally morbid fascination with such events? Or, is there something else there; something that cannot be seen on the big screen, or read from the pages of novels and scientific journals? And if so, what might it be?

James Cameron sought the answer to that question. In making the movie he wanted, "to live up to that level of reality" because it was not just a story or drama but, "...an event that happened to real people who really died." After viewing the wreck from inside a submersible for such a long time he, "...felt a strong sense of the profound sadness and injustice of it, and the message of it." He said, "...the magnificence of the great ship (was) matched in scale only by the folly of the men who drove her hell-bent through the darkness. And above all the lesson: that life is uncertain, the future unknowable...the unthinkable possible." ("Titanic" the book by James Cameron, 1998).

Though such words are cause for careful consideration, Cameron's best answer to the cause of the sinking was when he said the ship was destroyed by two things: an iceberg and a state of mind. In his book he speaks of "an unseen force that (would) ultimately lead to the era's downfall...arrogance". True, indeed.

An unknown commentator offered his opinion saying he felt that "Titanic" could not be properly controlled because of the small size of the rudder. Then he compared the ship to a world that could not be controlled as evidenced by the start of WW1 just two years after the sinking.

Those statements are noteworthy, but they are concerned only with what caused the tragedy. The underlying reason for the world's fascination with it is still not addressed. Some unusual reasons have been presented, but they are more amusing than realistic. For example: some people alive today are the reincarnated victims; people are constantly trying to re-live it in order to really know the feeling of being on a gigantic sinking ship; the disaster has an irresistible hypnotic power over people, etc.

With all such speculation aside, no one can argue against the real presence of something out there that will not allow

"Titanic" to be buried. Evidence of this strange association is plain. The world has no such fascination with "Andrea Doria" whose sinking had no logical explanation, or the civilian liner "Lusitania" which was sunk by a German torpedo in 1915. Add to that "Monitor", "Bismarck", "Edmond Fitzgerald" and many other famous sea disasters. Consider also that comparatively little interest exists regarding what some call the Bermuda Triangle mysteries. The fact is the "Titanic" disaster outdoes all of them, though the mechanics of the disaster are no more intriguing than those of similar catastrophes.

If that is true, what then is the answer, and does anybody really care what it might be? The fact is there is something that tethers generations to the sinking of "Titanic", and yes, many people are very interested. A number of scientists, journalists and arm-chair investigators would like to know why the world can't get beyond the event. For those who believe such disasters are not events disconnected from God's providence, the reason is indeed relevant. And, they also think it is not shrouded in some indecipherable lesson or message. It becomes plainly visible if honestly pursued.

Some readers might remember the 1958 movie about the "Titanic" titled, "A Night To Remember". In that movie Second Officer Charles Herbert Lightoller, the highest ranking officer to survive the sinking, made a statement at the end of the film saying they were all so sure about the safety of the ship that he, "will never be sure again, about anything." Did Lightoller unknowingly formulate what would quickly become Titanic's notorious and undying epitaph along with the reason future generations would not let it die? I think he came close.

The early 20th Century was filled with optimism and hope. Life was becoming more mechanized with manual labor requiring less sweat and effort with one result being more time for leisure and the pursuit of the mere joy of life. Many indulgencies here-to-fore available only to a few were becoming available to more people. Life expectancy had gone up from 37 years to 47 years since 1800. The sick-care professions went from the lethal philosophy of bloodletting to life-saving blood transfusions. Confidence in human intellect soared. Humanity seemed to be in control of its destiny. And, there was no end in sight. What a time to be alive!

Then the inconceivable happened. The fact that an iceberg, which in those waters should have been little more than an expected annoyance, could appear out of nowhere and so suddenly sink the inexpressibly grand and powerful "Titanic" was beyond reality. "Something is wrong...it just can't be...!" When disbelief succumbed to reality it left in its wake a fascination that has transcended a century. Why? Partly because the tragedy brought arrogant human competence face-to-face with its own mortality; that humanity is, indeed, not capable of controlling its destiny. But, there is more.

The events that caused the paths of the iceberg and "Titanic" to cross were, of course, visibly dissimilar. But, a deeper look shows there was indeed a connection. One came from the natural world; a world of physical elements that was subjected to a curse — the result of man's sin. The other came from the hearts of men; a storehouse of evil and self-serving intentions — also the result of man's sin. The easy part is admitting the natural world cannot control its destiny; the hard part is admitting the same for humanity. You see, mankind believes intellect governs cause and effect.

Details can only be guessed, but modern meteorology and oceanography provide some ironic information about the iceberg that put "Titanic" on the bottom. Though the great ship was only 5 years old from inception to sinking, the iceberg itself was over 3000 years old. It probably began with a snowfall on the western slopes of Greenland about the same time David was king of Israel. Once it broke off from Greenland in about 1910 it made its way into the Atlantic, something only about 1% of icebergs can accomplish. Usually they melt long before reaching that far south. By the beginning of WW1 it had disappeared, its fresh water having mixed anonymously with the vast seawater of the North Atlantic. It was forever gone leaving no trace at all. Ironically, one day "Titanic" herself will also be absorbed into that same seawater, leaving no trace of her existence much less evidence of her humanly-engineered opulence.

In essence Titanic's controllers placed the ship against forces whose presence and unforgiving lethality they ignored. Humanity, obviously, is tracking the same path. Though most people instinctively know something terrible is looming ahead, still the world proceeds recklessly at full speed ignoring every warning God has established. Humanists believe mankind has the ability, and even the manifest destiny to successfully confront life and everything it brings. All setbacks are seen only as "bumps in the road" — minor irritations that will eventually be handled through man's intellectual prowess and natural inclinations.

The White Star Line executives of 1912 refused to admit they were mere mortals smugly pursuing wealth, maritime speed records and fame in an environment whose powers they were unequipped to face. One hundred years later nothing has changed, and everybody intuitively knows it — that is the key to understanding why "Titanic" cannot be forgotten.

Beneath the thin veneer of confidence the world fearfully senses "Titanic" is a precursor to what is soon coming. The fascination is not only about the fact that the best man had to offer was not good enough in 1912, but is also about a constant and chilling premonition that man's best today is not good enough for what is about to show up on the doorstep.

Christians certainly should use perception and common sense regarding preparation for hard times, yet all in the context of knowing God will take the church out of the world prior to the tribulation. But, in our confidence we sometime fail to realize that unbelievers have no such assurance. They are really not at peace with what they see coming and how their leadership is responding to it. Deep down in their hearts many unbelievers are fearful of what they sense is about to happen. They are quite unnerved about what they believe could suddenly appear out of the fog.

Consider the "dooms-dayers". Their appraisal of what is coming is dead on, and many of their preparations are very commendable. Yet, because they do not know God's revealed plan they base their survival solely upon their own preparations and abilities. Regrettably, they have no hope beyond themselves.

Further, it is very, very interesting to hear them specifically list what they see coming. Most are expecting one or more of the following to happen: war (including local confrontations), famine and disease. Think about Revelation 6. The first rider is anti-Christ, and he is followed by what? War, famine and disease. Unknowingly, they fear what is actually going to happen. Does this not arrest our attention? Should not the fears many unbelievers have regarding what they specifically see as coming disasters and catastrophic human failure also be the reasons Christians are looking up in joyful expectation? The measures taken by those who will be left behind will prove to be about as effective as Titanic's water-tight compartments, even though they accurately foresee the unparalleled and ominous future.

Seemingly, the ghost of the lost ship haunts the human race, eerily appearing in its mirrors and dreams. Its unspoken, yet very obvious message is unmistakable: terrible judgment is at the bow, and humanity cannot escape it. DLM

Chapter 35

The Third Holy Temple

~ ~ ~ ~ ~

In God's mind the geo-religious center of the earth is Israel, and if an umbilical cord connecting heaven and the nation could be imagined it would terminate on the Temple Mount; a place of holiness in Judaism, and a place of great significance for Christians with a whetted sense of interest in prophecy. You see, in the not-so-distant future the Third Holy Temple will be erected on the Temple Mount in Jerusalem. This temple will be the one in existence during the tribulation, and that in itself makes it very interesting and relevant because multitudes alive today could very well see it. And not only might they see it, but they could also see the anti-Christ as he sets himself up as God in that same temple demanding world-wide worship. But, that will be nothing to look forward to, for life will be very uncertain in those days.

In the 4000 year history of the Jewish people there have been several buildings associated with God's presence. In the wilderness during their exodus from Egypt they constructed a tent, under the direction of God, called the Tabernacle. Due to wear-and-tear this tent took on several forms until David brought the Ark of the Covenant to Jerusalem and placed it into another tent. David wanted to build a permanent structure for the Ark, but was not allowed to do so. Instead, God allowed his son and successor Solomon to build a stone structure that was both astounding in its construction and magnificent in its appearance.

Solomon's Temple was destroyed by the Babylonians in 586 BC as the Jews were early into their 70 year exile. Later, under Cyrus, Zerubbabel returned to Jerusalem and went from the ground up with another temple that was finished in 516 BC. Over time that temple became the victim of deterioration and had, by the time of Herod the Great, become something unfit to be seen within the realm of such a master builder as he. Thus, Herod took on the monumental task of renovating the building. The result was a temple far more magnificent than the previous one. This, he felt, was only befitting of a king so architecturally talented as himself, and besides, it would serve as a sort of appeasement of the Jewish masses. Interestingly though, it has been argued that Herod's real purpose was to get hold of the royal Jewish genealogies kept in the temple complex in order to destroy any documents relating to the predicted coming of the Jewish Messiah, his perceived rival. Herod's temple was constantly being added to, and was finally completed only six years before its destruction by the Romans in AD 70.

From AD 70 until this very day the Jews have had no temple. Most in Christendom believe the entire temple issue is of no importance at all since the church, they say, has taken the place of Israel in God's blueprint for the world. They bolster their argument by pointing to the current presence of a Muslim shrine, The Dome of the Rock, standing upon the very spot where the temples of the past once stood. This, they believe, seals the deal, and any proposition that yet another temple will be constructed is simply outlandish at best and heretical at worse.

Those who take issue with the tribulation Temple base their conclusions upon several flawed assumptions. Foremost, they do not see Israel as being a legitimate nation with any kind of God-directed future. Next, they believe the general course of world events will continue in much the same way as they have for 2000 years. Put another way, they believe if human history could be plotted on a graph, then what is coming could be predicted simply by drawing a straight line from past day-to-day events to present day-to-day events and projecting that line into the future. They admit that Jesus will come someday, but surely not any time soon. His coming, they say, will catch Christians by surprise because, "no body knows the day". That is correct as far as it goes, but we can know the season of His return, and we have been advised to make ourselves aware of it. The doctrine of imminence innately instills an on-going expectation of the rapture.

Further, the issue-takers forget that on occasion God intervenes in the repetitive doldrums of life, thus abruptly re-directing the course of human history in extraordinary ways. If past events are to be used to project the future, then a more accurate projection might be based upon a line that connects those course-changing, unexpected "God events" of history instead of those predictable, mind-numbing routines of life.

Obviously, if the Jews are going to build another temple on the Temple Mount then something has to change the political and religious status quo. Said another way, Muslims will in no way allow the Temple to be built on the Mount, and no religious Jew would even consider building the Temple adjacent to pagan shrines presently on the Mount. This is gridlock of the most unyielding kind. Something must give, but no one knows exactly what it will be. God has a way of sometimes side-stepping human logic, and that means even though we know what will happen, it is impossible to make a detailed prediction regarding the means. That said, there are still some interesting things to consider about this matter of the Third Holy Temple.

Daniel 9:27 clearly indicates the 70th and final week of years (the tribulation) will begin with the coming prince (anti-Christ) brokering a covenant of some kind with Israel. There is no mention of the detailed pledges and bonds involved in the agreement, but it seems they will correlate with Israel's interests regarding her capital city of Jerusalem, and her being accepted among the nations of the world. Some believe anti-Christ will include the Temple in the negotiations in return for Israel practically dismantling her Israel Defense Forces. This scenario seems logical in light of Ezekiel 38:14. Plus, the Israeli government would be able to take the 6.9% of their GNP they spend on defense and invest it in technology and agriculture. Such an agreement would allow them to do just that. A problem with this argument is the continued presence of the Islamic shrines on the mount.

But, there is another issue that must be considered, and that is the fulfillment of Psalm 83 where Israel goes to war and decimates those Arab nations in close proximity to her borders. It seems to many prophecy students that nothing less than an all-out Israeli victory over the Islamic nations threatening her annihilation will bring resolution to the conflict, though temporary it will be. Such a victory would put Israel into a position where she could do as she pleases with the Temple Mount with no one to interfere. It might also include the destruction of the Islamic shrines. Additionally, seeing that the Arab hordes did not finished off the Jews in that war, the anti-Christ might then consider the treaty as a means to deceive Israel into disarming and placing her security into his hands (John 5:43). He would later use her complacency against her — about 3½ years later. This would require the Psalm 83 war to occur in nearness to the rapture.

Such scenarios, and others, are based upon speculation, with each one having both merits and liabilities. But, even speculation does not obscure the fact of the nearness of those events. There are two things that should give us pause each morning and each evening: it is a wonder that Jesus did not return that day or night, and it is a wonder that Israel is not at war.

Why the Third Holy Temple? The answer depends upon who is being asked. The Temple Institute, a private Jewish organization dedicated to preparing clothing, vessels, etc., for the new temple, believes that Judaism without the temple is like a fish out of water — it is unnatural. Further, its members want to see the Temple rebuilt for the spiritual wellbeing of not just Israel, but the entire world. They have an excellent grasp of Isaiah 56:7,8, but their timing is off.

If a prophecy-believing Christian is asked that question the answer will be rooted in the imminent return of Jesus. That Christian will understand how the signs pointing to Messiah Jesus' second coming to the earth (Matthew 24; Mark 13; Zechariah 14:4-9; Revelation 19:11ff) in effect point to the rapture because it happens seven years prior to the second coming. More precisely Jesus, in Matthew 24 and Mark 13, said the future would bring the fulfillment of a prophecy called "the abomination of desolation" initially introduced in Daniel 9:27; 11:31; 12:11. Most Christian scholars say that event was fulfilled by the Jew-hating Syrian Antiochus IV Epiphanes in 167 BC when he made a pagan sacrifice in the Jewish temple. However, 200 years later Jesus said it was future to His day, and His interpretation trumps that of the scholars every time.

The point, though, is that the soon-coming abomination of desolation will happen in a Jewish temple which is presently not in existence. And, in context of the signs Jesus talked about regarding His second coming, the only scriptural conclusion is it will be built in the near future. Though the means by which this will happen are unknown, many details regarding temple worship have already been managed.

Conversations often address the question of what will happen to the Islamic Dome of the Rock and Al Aqsa Mosque. Because that is unknown we should be content by simply knowing God sometimes does amazing things in bizarre ways.

The thing to keep in mind is the rapid unfolding of both worldwide and regional events that have Israel as their focal point. In the last newsletter it was pointed out that the peace treaties Israel has with Egypt and Jordan have digressed into something akin to mere cease-fire agreements. Since that time, Israel has closed her Embassy in Cairo in response to Egypt's growing animosity. In early March of 2012 Egypt's Islamist-controlled government demanded Israel's ambassador be expelled, and that the 1979 peace treaty be "reviewed", a code-word for annulled. The direction in which these events are going is obvious; the conclusion is equally obvious. The storm clouds of war have formed, and are only awaiting the saturation point. But, do not be afraid, for these events do not spell doom and gloom for Christians.

As with Belshazzar, this world has been weighed in the balance by God and found wanting. But, the Groom has promised to remove His bride before He delivers His strike. We rest in that. DLM

Chapter 36

Building the Tribulation GESTAPO

~ ~ ~ ~ ~

The greatest persecution of Jews during the 20th Century was the Holocaust of World War II. The German Third Reich developed and employed a tracking, apprehension, incarceration and killing machine that was used against millions of Jews and other undesirables during their "national emergency". The atrocities committed by the GESTAPO, the SS, the Einsaatzgruppen and other agencies of the state in the name of defense and security are unbelievable. The reality of what happened causes people even today to wonder how civilized people could be so cruel. After the depraved cruelty of the Nazis was clearly laid out in the Nuremberg trials, civilized humanity responded with a firmly intended, "Never again!". But, it will happen again, the perpetrators will again be civilized people, and a similar machine will be used.

On the other side of the world during that same period the Japanese were exercising the same cruelty with abandon. On December 13, 1937 troops of the Imperial Japanese Army captured Nanking, the then capital of the Republic of China. What followed was six weeks of ruthless brutality seldom seen even in times of war. Over 300,000 people were tortured in the most heinous of ways, beheaded, disemboweled, and even cannibalized. Rape, murder, looting, and every form of depravity imaginable were committed against civilians of both genders, of all ages including children, of unarmed Chinese soldiers, and anyone else who could be found. Though many records were destroyed by the Japanese and though denied by historical revisionists and many Japanese nationals, yet the evidence is there in pictures, written documentation and sworn testimony.

The East and the West, the Orient and the Occident — both hemispheric civilizations with histories of great accomplishments — digressed to a point that was not simply inhuman, but sub-human. Atrocities likened to the conduct of ravenous, mad animals were the day-to-day routines for what might be described as regular people, including those with wealth, education and social refinement.

So, has anything really changed? Have any lessons really been learned from those carnages? Have the war-crimes trials really created a world impervious to future slaughters? Has the United Nations really been able to prevent genocide or even conventional war? Is the human race now above such brutalities? Are all people-groups now protected from pogroms and ethnic cleansing? Obviously, the answer to all of the above is the same. No.

The use of coldblooded people in enslaving the masses for use as expendable property is no different today than it was in 1933 Germany, or in 1937 Japan. The only difference is technology has made the world smaller by making surveillance and control easier. When it comes to subjugating people, the framework of the past will support those more drastic actions that will come in response to future "national emergencies". Though enforcers in the future will cast aside the brown shirts and black uniforms, yet ice water will surge through their veins. Further, the removal of the church will open the way for unprecedented and unrestrained government-sanctioned oppression of all "enemies of the state".

The result of the irreparably evil global heart will be God's judgment upon the post-rapture world. It will begin with anti-Christ signing some kind of treaty with Israel, and it will end with Jesus Christ's second coming to this earth. The time frame will be seven years and during that period, "the great tribulation" as Jesus called it, several eventualities will unfold: anti-Christ will direct the murder of multitudes, everyone will be someone's enemy, and the Jews will be everyone's enemy. Carnage will eventually be the order of the day with headlines of bloody events possibly leading many news broadcasts. The brutality of Imperial Japan and Nazi Germany will be overshadowed by the barbarism of the New World Order.

Most Christians have a tendency to give only a cursory nod to those eventualities. But others are captivated by these things, and often pause to give some thought to not only the events, but to the players. With death by blood-letting being common in those days (Revelation 6:4), they ask a familiar question about the perpetrators. That is, who would be capable of not only having no regard for life, but who would get enjoyment from being part of the butchery? The answer echoes from the 1930s: regular, civilized people will morph into savages once again.

The men (and some women) who carried out the Nazi atrocities were not blood-thirsty criminals, as many modern readers believe. Simon Wiesenthal, survivor of Hitler's death camps and famous Nazi hunter, lent support to this idea with his comment about their not being criminals. Wiesenthal said, "The National Socialist (Nazi) party had 10 million members, of whom at most 150,000 were criminals. It would be grotesque to stick the label of criminal on every former member of the party." (brainyquote.com) It is very difficult to believe that those who burned women and children alive in synagogues had no criminal history; that they were what many would call "normal people", but they were.

In his book, "Ordinary Men: Reserve Police Battalion 101 and the Final Solution in Poland", Christopher Browning points out that the battalion commander gave his men the option of not serving in the death squads if they found such duty to be "unpleasant". Of the 500 men in the battalion only 15 opted out. He further states that they were not Nazi fanatics, but ordinary working-class, middle-aged men from Hamburg. Browning concluded that ordinary people in a coherent group will likely follow orders, even questionable orders, if issued by an authority. "Just following orders", as you might remember, was a defense argument at the Nuremberg trials. The court, of course, rejected it.

Certainly a sizeable number of Germans were not Nazis, did not subscribe to genocide, did not participate in mass murder, etc. Though that is true, yet that is not the point. The point is that many of the men who butchered men, women and children were pre-war clerks, physicians, bureaucrats, accountants, merchants, attorneys, truck drivers, etc. They provided for their families, were faithful husbands, tax-payers, supporters of the arts and demonstrated no decisive pre-war evidence that they could become animals whose prey would be fellow humans. They were simply normal people.

With that as something of a groundwork, it becomes easier to see how there is not, and will never be a shortage of people willing to enforce the laws and carry out the orders of any police state. Jesus pointed directly to this when He said to the Jews that a time is coming when friends and even family members will betray each other (Matthew 24:9, 10; Luke 21:16) This is strong evidence as to who will constitute the soon-coming re-creation of the Nazi GESTAPO.

This agency will probably be regional in its early stages, but will become a global organization at its zenith. Such a change will be necessary because independent national bureaus will not be trustworthy enough for anti-Christ due to inherent national loyalties. Its global authority and plenary power will possibly come into its own about the same time anti-Christ expropriates the Jewish Temple and demands global worship. He will place the jack-boot of merciless totalitarianism on the necks of all people, beheading any who might resist. He will then begin his systematic effort to completely destroy the Jewish people in a campaign that will amount to the final, "Final Solution to the Jewish Question". In his unbridled spree to subjugate the world and annihilate any resistance no stone will be left unturned. No mercy will be shown and no excuses will be accepted. His minions will be terse and shameless as they delve into the private details of people's lives.

Official and callous abruptness will accompany the words, "Your papers, please." People will think, "I can't believe it...he was such a nice boy growing up." Fear of family and neighbors and the complete absence of trust will add to the emotional trauma of the tribulation. The horrifying judgments that will disrupt every normal aspect of life coupled with fear of friends and neighbors will add crippling strain to an already unbearable situation. Nothing in history can compare.

Many countries presently have agencies that oversee most every aspect of their citizen's lives. For those countries the next major step will be consolidation into anti-Christ's global agency. Other nations are near the threshold of such control, and the Islamic threat has been a golden gift on a silver platter to those pursuing that agenda in those heretofore free nations.

A growing number of Americans see their government going in that direction, but Christians do not see it so much as a liberal/conservative issue as much as they see it as a spiritual battle. The 20th Century was a critical time in Satan's efforts at usurping God's plan for this earth, and the last several decades have been a boon to him. As was the case with Cyrus, king of Persia in Daniel 10, he is attempting to manipulate the American political agenda by stealth, and he has been quite successful. And, America's politically correct response to the Islamic threat is tailor-made for his efforts.

The growing number of American bureaus dedicated solely to national security is one of Satan's greatest achievements mainly because this "security bureaucracy" could likely be the foundation for a future federal police agency that will eclipse anything presently on the books. Perhaps surprisingly, this has nothing to do with conspiracies; its roots go much deeper than the mere topsoil of human ambition. Rather, it has everything to do with Satan's efforts to lay the foundation for one man, his man, to be ushered into global power. He is building the scenario, one step, and one agency at a time while patiently waiting for the right moment. Such an organization, he believes, will be necessary for keeping his anti-Christ in a virtually incontestable position of power.

Part of his plan to take this world for his own domain requires that there be in place a post-rapture enforcement agency whose agents have no squeamish feelings about dealing with those who might resist. As is the case in modern enforcement agencies, some will be wholly dedicated idealists, while others will look at it simply as a job. In either case, though, most of them will be regular, normal people. However, they will view those who resist their new leader's overtures as "enemies of the state", and not qualified to be citizens of the new world order. Much in the same way the Japanese military viewed the Chinese and Koreans, and the way Nazis viewed the Jews and other "lower life forms" unworthy of the Fuhrer's Reich.

A careful look at the present global status reveals more than the obvious manipulation of nations and economies, and more than the growing instability of the Middle East. It reveals what appears to be a popular governmental inclination toward enforcement agencies that will be indispensable for the imposition of control through martial law, intimidation and terror. Ostensibly, the purpose of such agencies, at least in the U.S., will be to respond to national emergencies, a somewhat vague term in itself. With modern security organizations regularly ignoring the U.S. Constitution with impunity, America appears to be well on her way to accepting such activity as a normal part of post 9-11 life.

The final product will be something along the lines of the Nazi GESTAPO, only with greater ability to control the masses than the Nazis had. And, it will be those regional agencies with their own enforcers that will be consolidated into a global unit that swears allegiance to the new Fuhrer instead of swearing allegiance to a written constitution. No one knows if it will be a natural disaster, Islamic attack, pandemic disease or economic collapse that will make such an agency operational in our country, but certainly the rapture of the church and the resulting chaos would do it. DLM